W9-BUZ-589

It's on the
Tip of My Tongue

Other Titles by Diane J. German, PhD

Test of Word Finding, Second Edition (TWF–2)
Word Finding Intervention Program (WFIP)
Test of Adolescent/Adult Word Finding (TAWF)
Test of Word Finding In Discourse (TWFD)
Word Finding Referral Checklist (WFRC)

It's on the Tip of My Tongue

Word-Finding Strategies to Remember Names and Words You Often Forget

Diane J. German, PhD
National-Louis University

WORD FINDING MATERIALS, INC.

Copyright © 2001 by Diane J. German
All rights reserved. No part of this publication may be reproduced,
stored in a retrieval system, or transmitted, in any form or by any
means, electronic, mechanical, photocopying, recording, or
otherwise, without the prior written permission of Diane J. German.

Editors: Melanie A. Bartels Graw and Barbara J. Wendling
Design: Matthew Doherty Design
Production: Burkeline

Manufactured in the United States of America
Library of Congress Control Number: 00 – 136692

German, Diane J.
    It's on the tip of my tongue : word-finding
strategies to remember names and words you often forget
/ Diane J. German. — 1st ed.
    p. cm.
    Includes bibliographical references and index.
    LCCN: 00–136692
    ISBN 0–9705103–0–6

    1. Mnemonics. 2. Memory. 3. Human information
processing. I. Title.

BF385.G47 2001   153.1'4
                                        QBI00–1041

Word Finding Materials, Inc.
P.O. Box 64456
Chicago, IL 60664–0456
Phone/fax 1–866–808–5290
http://www.word-finding.com

10 9 8 7 6 5 4 3 2 1   UG   01 02 03 04 05

To Arthur E. German,
Thank you for your forever support and commitment
to my work in Word Finding. For it is together that I am able
to make this contribution to individuals everywhere in hopes
that it will improve their word finding skills.

What Individuals Say About
It's on the Tip of My Tongue

In her user-friendly text, Dr. German clearly identifies different types of word-finding difficulties, and more importantly, what we can do about them. Teens and older adults who struggle with these problems as well as their families, teachers, and friends will welcome this informative and practical guide that encourages us to take control of our memory for words.

Bonnie E. Litowitz, PhD
Associate Professor, Department of Psychiatry
Rush Medical School

The word-finding difficulties of high school and university students are often overlooked. Yet these difficulties often interfere with students' writing and verbal communication. The book *It's on the Tip of My Tongue,* provides LD teachers and speech and language professionals with a wealth of strategies for assisting students in coping with their word-finding difficulties. The book is easy to read, provides many useful illustrations, and includes icons and graphics to help the reader.

Janet W. Lerner, PhD
Professor Emeritus, Department of Special Education
Northeastern Illinois University
Author of *Learning Disabilities, Theories, Diagnosis, and Teaching Strategies.*

Diane German's book is a thorough and helpful guide for addressing word-finding problems. I found the examples and diagnosis to be especially helpful so that I could target my personal word-finding difficulties. Most of all, this book gives me hope that there is help for my word-finding difficulties. In addition, as a teacher, the strategies will help me support children with word-finding difficulties in my classroom.

Diane Deckert
Associate Professor, Baker Demonstration School
National-Louis University

Table of Contents

FOREWORD

by Geraldine P. Wallach, PhD CCC-SLP
Associate Professor, Department of Communicative Disorders
California State University, Long Beach

Have you ever forgotten a person's name at the moment of introduction? Ever struggled in the middle of a conversation to recall the name of the town where your friends just bought a new condo? Ever attempt to pronounce a complex word only to substitute a word that sounds similar, but falls short of the intended target? Ever lose a seemingly familiar word suddenly? All speakers of a language—young and old, professional and nonprofessional, male and female (including all other categories one might use to describe the human condition)—can identify with these phenomena. Communication, among the most basic yet critical aspects of human endeavors, is often taken for granted until it is lost or disrupted. To say the least, losing words and struggling to find them, can be embarrassing and frustrating. Word-finding lapses cannot only interrupt one's train of thought and enthusiasm for lively conversation, but these lapses can also contribute to feelings of self-doubt and anxiety. Luckily, help is on the way!

Dr. Diane German, a consummate researcher, teacher, clinician, and nationally-recognized scholar in the area of word finding and retrieval, presents her readers with a book that is extremely well organized. It is clever and timely, packaging for its readers research-based concepts in very accessible and user-friendly ways. The book presents readers with an excellent summary of the nature and types of word-finding difficulties that may occur in everyday conversations, in workplace situations and within classroom settings. Through a series of cartoon-like "conversation bubbles," German gives readers examples of word-finding errors they may be experiencing. The book not only provides readers with information about the different types of word-finding problems, it also provides them with detailed self-evaluation checklists to help readers identify their own word-finding errors. Dr. German guides her readers through the book with creative icons that serve as friendly road maps, or bookmarks, through discussion sections and to the practical how's, when's, and why's of word naming and retrieval improvements. The self-evaluation section is particularly interesting—readers might enjoy comparing their findings with family and friends who may also be experiencing word-finding difficulties. Indeed, this is far from a "one size fits all" book. German is careful to point out both the "do's" and "don'ts" of particular word-finding strategies and is cautious about the recommendations she makes for readers. Her carefully-crafted strategic approach to self-monitoring and self-awareness helps readers focus on what might be significant areas for improvement. By demonstrating how different "tips" work for different people, we get a better understanding of the complexity of word-finding difficulties. We also understand how association strategies might work for one person, whereas pausing strategies might work better for another person.

This book is timely from many perspectives. This book would be extremely useful for our senior citizens, who are vibrant and living longer than ever, but who certainly have experienced some of the "lost words" German discusses. This book would also be very valuable to those of us, myself included, who are part of the "baby boomer" generation and who are losing more words daily than we would like to admit. This book would be a useful addition to the libraries of adolescents and university students who might have difficulty with classroom and academic learning. For all of us, embarking on this age of ever-changing technology, learning and retaining the new twenty-first century lexicon may certainly present some challenges. No doubt, having specific strategies to improve our memory for retrieval of words would be welcomed.

Readers will enjoy the adventure into the world of words that German has outlined. Steeped in over twenty years of research, Dr. German shares her wealth of knowledge with her readers. While accessible and easy to follow, with pages and pages of practical suggestions for improving word-finding skills, readers will go back for several readings and will, no doubt, use the book as a great reference source. *It's on the Tip of My Tongue* is intelligent, fun, mind stretching, thorough, creative, and exciting. There are probably more words to describe what German provides for her readers—it is for the reader to find the appropriate words after his or her own exploration.

INTRODUCTION

Has this ever happened to you?

- You call someone by his or her brother's name. For example, "Joe, I mean Leo, it is good to see you."

- You stop in the middle of a conversation because you cannot think of a word. For example, "This spring our yard is full of…."

- At a party, you introduce someone you know and mispronounce their name. For example, "I want you to meet Barbara Beclachm…Beth-Halac…."

If these examples remind you of your own language, then you may be making word-finding errors when you are talking. If so, this book is for you.

The Purpose of this Book

This book provides you with memory strategies to improve your word-finding skills. Word-finding skills refer to your ability to select or retrieve known words from your memory. In other words, it is your ability to remember and call to mind those words you want to say when speaking.

Why this Book Is for You

Learning memory strategies to improve word-finding skills is beneficial for individuals of any age. Using these strategies will improve your communication skills with your family, friends, coworkers, and teachers. It will help you eliminate those embarrassing gaps or errors in conversations. In general, applying these strategies at home, at community and social events, at work, and at school will help you to become a better communicator, speaker, and learner.

So pat yourself on the back; you are in control! By reading this book, you have begun the process of improving your memory for words and names. As you apply the strategies in this book to the words you are having difficulty retrieving you will be engaging in "strategic intervention." Through intervention you will improve your word-finding skills and take control of your memory for words.

What You Will Learn about Your Word Finding

You will gain a new understanding of your memory system for words and names. You will learn memory strategies that can improve your word-finding abilities. Specifically, you will learn to

- identify three types of word-finding difficulties;
- evaluate your word-finding skills;
- identify the type of word-finding difficulties you display;
- use strategies to reduce the occurrence of each of these types of word-finding difficulties;
- improve your word-finding skills for specific types of names and words; and
- create plans and accommodations to improve your word finding skills in social, academic, and work settings.

How this Book Differs from Other Memory Books

Many good books about memory discuss strategies to help individuals remember new names (Higbee, 1993; Lorayne & Lucas, 1974; Trudeau, 1995). Further, other good sources provide memory strategies for remembering lists, definitions, and facts (Deshler, Ellis, & Lenz, 1996; Mastropieri & Scruggs, 1991). In contrast, the primary focus of this book is on memory strategies to improve your language skills. The goal of this book is to improve your word-finding skills while engaged in conversations or discussions. Specifically, it provides word-finding strategies to improve your retrieval of names and words that you already know and have recalled correctly in other contexts. In addition, this book includes chapters with strategies to improve word-finding skills of learned vocabulary in academic and work settings and presents suggestions for accommodations in these settings that will aid your word finding.

Organization of this Book

Each of the chapters in this book provides you with important information about your word-finding skills.

Chapter 1 introduces you to the memory process of word finding. A definition of word finding and word-finding difficulties is presented, types and characteristics of word-finding difficulties are described, and conditions contributing to word-finding difficulties are indicated. Additionally, eight rules for successful improvement in word finding are highlighted.

Chapter 2 defines the three most common types of word-finding errors: "Slip of the Tongue," "Tip of the Tongue" experiences, and "Twist of the Tongue." Examples of each of these word-finding errors are presented.

Chapter 3 includes a Word-Finding Questionnaire that will help you to evaluate your word-finding skills. This self-evaluation will help you to become familiar with the word-finding characteristics that are typical of your speaking patterns. It will also help you to determine what types of word-finding errors you typically produce when you are speaking.

Chapter 4 describes word-finding strategies, presents the steps involved in applying each strategy, and matches these strategies to the different types of word-finding errors.

Chapter 5 presents a list that can help you successfully handle those situations when you make a "Slip of the Tongue" word-finding error.

Chapter 6 presents word-finding strategies to reduce "Slips of the Tongue" with known names of family members, friends, and coworkers; with specific names of places, events or entities; and with common words.

Chapter 7 provides final guidelines for using the word-finding strategies to reduce "Slips of the Tongue" when you are speaking.

Chapter 8 presents a list that can help you successfully handle those situations when you have a "Tip of the Tongue" experience.

Chapter 9 presents word-finding strategies to reduce "Tip of the Tongue" word-finding errors with known names of family members, friends, and coworkers; with specific names of places, events, or entities; and with common words.

Chapter 10 provides final guidelines for using the word-finding strategies to reduce "Tip of the Tongue" experiences when you are speaking.

Chapter 11 presents a list that can help you successfully handle those situations when you make a "Twist of the Tongue" word-finding error.

Chapters 12 presents word-finding strategies to reduce "Twist of the Tongue" word-finding errors with known names of family members, friends, and coworkers; with specific names of places, events, or entities; and with common words.

Chapter 13 provides final guidelines for using the word-finding strategies to reduce "Twists of the Tongue" when you are speaking.

Chapter 14 provides plans to guide your preparation for speaking events at family and social functions that may put a high demand on your word-finding system.

Chapter 15 provides plans to guide your preparation for speaking events in business, community, or school settings;

making presentations and speeches; and asking questions and discussing topics at meetings.

Chapter 16 illustrates how to apply word-finding strategies to aid your retrieval of academic- and work-related vocabulary.

Chapter 17 provides recommendations for accommodations in academic and work settings that may put a high demand on your word-finding system.

Icons to Guide Your Use of this Book

Throughout this book, icons are used to mark material that is especially important to you.

 This icon marks examples of "Slip of the Tongue" word-finding errors.

 This icon marks examples of "Tip of the Tongue" word-finding errors.

 This icon marks examples of "Twist of the Tongue" word-finding errors.

 This icon marks retrieval strategies. Application of retrieval strategies is the key to successful word finding.

 This icon indicates the steps to follow when applying word-finding strategies.

 This icon indicates when to use the word-finding strategies.

 This icon indicates additional reading resources for more information.

PART 1

Getting Started– What You Should Know about Word Finding

Definitions of Word Finding and Word-Finding Difficulties

This chapter presents important information about word finding that will ultimately help you to improve your word-finding skills. Word finding is defined and three types of word-finding errors are described. The following questions are addressed.

- What is word finding?
- What are word-finding difficulties?
- What are characteristics of word-finding difficulties?
- Under what circumstances can you have word-finding difficulties?
- What are the rules for successful improvement of your word-finding skills?

What Is Word Finding?

Word finding refers to the mental activity of selecting or retrieving from your memory words that you know, to express what you want to say.

What Are Word-Finding Difficulties?

A word-finding difficulty is a disruption in the mental activity of retrieving known words from your memory. When this disruption occurs you have difficulty finding (retrieving) word(s) or name(s) that you want to say (German, 1990). You may want to address a person or refer to an individual or place that you have in mind. You know the name or word, but you cannot select or retrieve it from your memory when you want to say it. You either misspeak, pause in silence, or mispronounce the target word.

Higbee (1993) distinguishes between information in memory that is available and information that is accessible. *Available* information is material that you know and that is stored in your memory. *Accessible* information is available material that can be recalled or retrieved. He indicates that it is possible to have available information (material you know), that is not accessible (you cannot recall or retrieve it). This occurs when you have a word-finding difficulty. You know the word (it is available in your memory), but you cannot always retrieve it (it is not accessible) for usage.

Generally, although not exclusively, there are three types of word-finding difficulties that you can experience. They may occur in isolation or in combination. For purposes of this book each of these word-finding difficulties is discussed separately. They are introduced here and described in more detail in Chapter 2.

A "Slip of the Tongue" – Word Substitution

Pass me the mustard, I mean ketchup!

You may sometimes produce a "Slip of the Tongue" and say the wrong word.

A "Tip of the Tongue" – Lost Word

I want you to meet... what is her name?

Other times you may experience a name on the "Tip of Your Tongue." You know it, but you cannot retrieve it.

A "Twist of the Tongue" – Word Attempt

Did you celebrate the milenum at home?

Or you may experience a "Twist of the Tongue" and mispronounce the word (e.g., say "milenum" when you mean to say *millennium*).

Characteristics of Word-Finding Difficulties

When you are having difficulty retrieving words you know, you may demonstrate behavioral characteristics that are typical of slips (word substitutions), tips (lost words), or twists (word attempts) of the tongue.

"Slip of the Tongue" Characteristics

Interchange the names of individuals who are related to each other or similarly related to the speaker.

Substitute an interfering word that is often said with other words in the sentence.

Substitute an interfering word that sounds like the word you are trying to find (e.g., ask for "sauce" when you want *sausage*).

"Tip of the Tongue" Characteristics

Oh…what is that answer? I know that.

Have a long delay while you are trying to think of a known answer to a question and then find that you remember the word later in the conversation.

Snap your fingers in frustration as you search your mind for an elusive word.

It's um…uh…it's used to check your heart beat.

Vocalize time fillers such as "um" or "uh" as you try to think of the target word (e.g., say, "It's…um…uh…" while you search your mind for the word *stethoscope*).

"Twist of the Tongue" Characteristics

Do you like bordaise sauce?

Omit syllables of words that are three or more syllables in length (e.g., say "bordaise" for the word *bordelaise*).

I am going to have a Mig Bac for lunch.

Exchange sounds of words that are frequently said together (e.g., say "Mig Bac" for *Big Mac*) or of acronyms that are three or more letters in length (e.g., say "YK2" for *Y2K*).

> **My colleague is Dr. Marski... Marinski.**

Mispronounce the name of a colleague that is three or more syllables in length (e.g., say "Dr. Marski" for *Dr. Marinski*).

Circumstances When You Can Have Word-Finding Difficulties

A word-finding difficulty can occur when you need to say only one or two words or when you are selecting many words in a conversation. Although a word-finding difficulty can occur with any part of speech, at any time, it usually occurs with those words that are the most important in conveying your message. For example, you will probably have word-finding difficulties with names when it is most important for you to remember those names. It may occur when you are addressing the person, referring to the person, or introducing the person to someone else. Word-finding difficulties may occur when you are

- Trying to find or retrieve a person's name—a friend, a child, a grandchild, or an author of a book.
- Trying to find or retrieve the name of a location—a street name, a city name, or the name of a building.
- Trying to find or retrieve the title of a book, a movie, or the name of a document.
- Trying to find or retrieve the name of a product—the name of a vitamin, a food, a medication, a tool, or some other object.

Rules for Successful Improvement of Your Word-Finding Skills

You need to embrace the following eight rules to succeed in improving your word-finding skills.

Rule 1: Do Not Be Afraid; You Are Not Alone!

Working to improve your memory for names and words may be a new experience for you, but it is not a new concept. Authors have written about the importance of applying techniques to improve one's memory for many years (Higbee, 1993; Lorayne & Lucas, 1974; Mastropieri & Scruggs, 1991; Parenté & Herrmann, 1996; Pressley & Woloshyn, 1995; Trudeau, 1995). By deciding to improve your memory for finding words, you have become a member of an enlightened group of people who understand the importance of taking care of their memory.

Rule 2: Fight the Feeling!

Fight the feeling that you cannot improve your word-finding skills. Feel empowered and believe that you can improve your word-finding skills by using the word-finding strategies in this book. Although it will take some effort to apply the strategies, remember that the strength of your memory could be more a function of the strategies you use than a function of any innate capacity you may have (Higbee, 1993).

Rule 3: Stay Focused—Become a Caretaker of Your Memory for Names and Words.

First, identify the nature of your word-finding difficulties through the self-evaluation methods suggested in this book. Second, select the word-finding strategies that will help you improve your word-finding skills. Third, apply these word-finding strategies to different types of words and names that you have difficulty retrieving.

Rule 4: Even Though You Know Names and Words, You May Still Need Strategies to Successfully Use Them!

Remember that even though you have stored material in your memory, the material may not be accessible (Higbee, 1993). Therefore, even though you know the names and words that you are having difficulty saying, you may still need to apply word-finding strategies to consistently retrieve them correctly.

Rule 5: You Can Predict the Future!

You can predict many of the words and names that you will need to remember in upcoming situations. Typically, you know who is going to be at a party or event that you are attending. Rehearse the names of these people before you will need to retrieve the names. Similarly, you can often predict the current events that are going to be discussed or the topics that will be of interest to the attending guests. Therefore, prior to the event, identify and rehearse the names and words you will need to be prepared to talk about the current events or topics of discussion.

Rule 6: If at First You Do Not Succeed, Try Again!

If you are still having difficulty with a particular word after you have applied a word-finding strategy, rehearse the strategy again or apply a second strategy. It may take more than one attempt or more than one strategy to anchor retrieval of some words.

Rule 7: Remember, Practice Makes Perfect!

Using the word-finding strategies, practice and rehearse target words that are important to you. With practice, it will become easier for you to apply the strategies and become automatic in retrieving target words.

Rule 8: Do Not Get Discouraged—Stay Positive!

Stay positive about improving your word-finding skills. The more you focus on applying your word-finding strategies, the easier word finding will be for you. Like flossing, watching your diet, and exercising, you will always need to apply word-finding strategies to your language. However, through frequent use of the strategies you can improve your word-finding skills.

Types of Word-Finding Errors

In Chapter 1 you were introduced to three types of word-finding errors.

- Type 1: "Slip of the Tongue"–Word Substitution
- Type 2: "Tip of the Tongue"–Lost Word
- Type 3: "Twist of the Tongue"–Word Attempt

Each of these word-finding error types are discussed in more detail in this chapter. Examples are provided to help you recognize these different word-finding errors. The following questions are addressed.

- What are the three different types of word-finding errors?
- What are examples of each type of word-finding error?

A "Slip of the Tongue"–Word Substitution

"Slips of the Tongue" refer to those occasions when one misspeaks and substitutes an interfering word for the target word.

"Slips of the Tongue" are commonly called "bloopers." Typically, these errors are word substitutions related to the meaning or sound form of the target word (Fromkin, 1973). The following are brief descriptions of different "Slip of the Tongue" errors.

Meaning Error

One word is substituted for another word because they are both said frequently with other words in the sentence (Roelofs, 1993).

Please turn off the light bulb.

In this example, instead of saying the target word *switch* with the word *light* (as in light switch), the interfering word *bulb* was said because it too is said frequently with the word *light* (as in light bulb).

Similarly, one proper noun may be substituted for another proper noun when addressing people by their names. In these situations a different name interferes with selection of the target name. Usually the interfering names belong to individuals who have similar relationships to the speaker or are themselves related. For example, a mother may substitute one daughter's name for another's.

> *Cindy...*
> *Ann please*
> *call me later.*

In this example, the mother called her daughter Ann by her other daughter's name, Cindy. In this situation speakers will often self-correct their "Slips of the Tongue."

Sound-Form Error

> *Good luck,*
> *I wish you a*
> *memorial*
> *experience.*

Another "Slip of the Tongue" error can be due to an interfering word that consists of some of the same sounds as the target word (Fay & Cutler, 1977).

In this example, the speaker retrieved the word *memorial* instead of the target word *memorable*. *Memorial* shares some of the same sounds as the target word *memorable* but does not share the same meaning. Interfering words that share some of the same sounds as the target word, but are not related to the target word in meaning, are also called "malapropisms" (Levelt, 1989).

For Further Reading

The "Slip of the Tongue" word-finding error was originally studied by Fromkin (1973, 1980) and Fay and Cutler (1977). Subsequently, many researchers have studied this type of speech error. For more information about the characteristics of the "Slip of the Tongue" word-finding error, consult Butterworth (1980, 1981, 1989, 1993), Garrett (1993), Levelt (1989, 1993), and Roelofs (1993).

"Slip of the Tongue" Examples

Following are different examples of "Slips of the Tongue." Put an X in the That's Me box under the examples that remind you of word-finding errors that you make. This practice section will prepare you for the more detailed self-evaluation of your word finding skills in Chapter 3.

Meaning Error

Please pick up my prescription at Walgreens.

In this example, the speaker misspoke and said "Walgreens" when she meant to say *Osco*. Because Walgreens also has a pharmacy, it interfered with selection of the target name Osco.

Sound-Form Error

You look impeachable today.

In this example, the word *impeachable* interfered with selection of the word *impeccable*. These words consist of some of the same sounds.

Sound-Form Error

The country is emergency.

In this example, the word *emergency* interfered with retrieval of the target word *emerging*. These words also consist of some of the same sounds.

Sound-Form Error

Sometimes I think he has ESPN.

In this example, the acronym *ESPN* interfered with retrieval of the target acronym *ESP*. These acronyms consist of some of the same sounds.

Meaning Error

Florence... Frances...Ethel is coming to visit me.

The names Florence and Frances interfered with retrieval of the target name, Ethel, because these individuals are all daughters of the speaker.

Following are other "Slips of the Tongue" reported by individuals like yourself. Continue to think about your own word-finding skills as you read these examples. If you have ever produced a "Slip of the Tongue" word-finding error similar to the example, enter an X in the That's Me column. Many X's in this column suggest that you have had "Slips of the Tongue" when you failed to retrieve a word or name.

A "Tip of the Tongue"–Lost Word

The "Tip of Tongue" phenomenon occurs when the retrieval of a word is temporarily not possible, but is believed to be imminent. You have the word in mind, but you cannot say it.

Target Word	"Slip of the Tongue" Examples	That's Me
candles	"Blow out your birthday cake...candles."	○
show dog	"She is considered a show girl...show dog."	○
good traits	"He does have some very good treats."	○
sabbatical	"Did you do this before you went on vacation, I mean sabbatical?"	○
phone number	"My address is 555-1212."	○
salad	"Do you want lettuce?"	○
Jesse Jackson	"Michael Jackson is a great speaker."	○
degree	"Did she earn a graduate course?"	○
aspersions	"You shouldn't cast spells."	○

Speakers having "Tip of the Tongue" experiences say that target words are so elusive they feel as if their minds have gone blank. Other speakers can only produce the first sound, or tell the number of syllables, and syllabic stress of a target word (Brown & McNeill, 1966). However, most of these individuals are able to retrieve the elusive word when they are prompted with its first sound or syllable (Nicholas, Barth, Obler, Au, & Albert, 1997).

One explanation for not being able to retrieve a word in these situations is that you are having difficulty finding the sounds that make up that word. Although you may remember the first sound of the word or the number of syllables of the word, you are not able to retrieve the entire word. This may cause a long delay before saying the word or you may not remember the word until you hear the listener say it. Sometimes speakers describe the function of the word that they cannot find. For example, one individual said for travel agency: "It is a shop that is like a book shop, but sells holidays." In these situations, speakers feel that they will retrieve the word at a later point in time even though they cannot think of the word at the moment.

For Further Reading

The "Tip of the Tongue" state was originally studied by Brown and McNeill (1966). Subsequently their procedures for studying "Tip of the Tongue" experiences in typical individuals has been used by many researchers. For more information about the characteristics of the "Tip of the Tongue" state, consult Bock and Levelt (1994); Burke, MacKay, Worthley, and Wade (1991); Butterworth (1980, 1981, 1989, 1993); Caramazza and Hillis, (1991); Jones (1989); Jones and Langford (1987); Koriat and Lieblich (1974); Meyer and Bock (1992); Nicholas, Barth, Obler, Au, and Albert (1997); and Semenza (1997).

I need the ...um...doohickey ...to serve the chicken.

A "Tip of the Tongue" experience may occur with an object name. In this situation, the speaker substituted "doohickey" for tongs because he was not able to retrieve the target word in the sentence, "I need the *tongs* to serve the chicken."

The "Tip of the Tongue" experience may also occur with a person's name. In this situation, the speaker said, "um…uh" and her response was delayed because she could not retrieve the target name in the sentence: "The principal's name is Dr. McCarthy."

The "Tip of the Tongue" experience may also occur with a descriptive word (adjective). In this situation, the speaker had a long delay because he was unable to retrieve the target adjective in the sentence: "He is such a personable guy."

The "Tip of the Tongue" experience may also occur with the action word (verb) in the sentence. In this example, the speaker was not able to find the target verb in the sentence: "He is organizing the entire event."

Individuals report that they may have a "Tip of the Tongue" experience when trying to retrieve

- names of family members, friends, coworkers, book authors;
- names of places that they have visited;
- names of movies that they have seen;
- names of books that they have read;
- names of objects that they know;
- adjectives that they have said before; and
- action words in sentences.

"Tip of the Tongue" Examples

Following are examples of what individuals have said when having a "Tip of the Tongue" experience. Continue the informal evaluation of your own word-finding skills, by putting an X in the That's Me box if the word-finding behavior is typical of you when you are having difficulty finding a word.

In this conversation, the word was so elusive that the speaker asked for help.

In this conversation, the word was so elusive that the speaker claimed defeat.

In this conversation, the speaker substituted the indefinite pronoun *thing*, for the word he was unable to retrieve, *warranty*.

> *The star of* **Forrest Gump** *was...um...oh; what's his name?*

In this conversation, the speaker had a "Tip of the Tongue" experience with the name of an actor that he knew, Tom Hanks.

That's Me ○

> *The author of* *the* **War Prayer** *is...um...he is well-known.*

In this conversation, the speaker could not retrieve the name of the well-known author, Mark Twain.

That's Me ○

Continue to think about your own word-finding skills as you read the following examples. If you have ever experienced a "Tip of the Tongue" word-finding error similar to the example, enter an X in the That's Me column. Many X's in this column suggest that you have had "Tip of the Tongue" experiences when you failed to retrieve a word or name.

Target Word	"Tip of the Tongue" Examples	That's Me
rotisserie	"Do you use the thing-a-ma-jig when you make the chicken?"	○
John Grisham	"I just finished reading his last book…oh…um…I just…what is his name?"	○
Al	"Yes, I am calling to speak to…um…uh…the owner of Vascos."	○
Michael Jordan	"For me, the best basketball player will always be…um…not Jackson…."	○
artichokes	"I am going to pick up pineapple, onions, and…um…um…um…what is it called?"	○
poinsettia	"I am going to buy my neighbor a…red flower for Christmas."	○
Matsuyas	"Let's meet at…at…um…um…the Japanese restaurant on Clark Street."	○
ethernet	"You need two…um…uh…not internet…but…two…ports."	○
stapler	"Has anyone seen the…fastener?"	○

A "Twist of the Tongue"–Word Attempt

"Twists of the Tongue" refer to those occasions when you omit or exchange sounds or syllables of long names or words that you know and have previously said correctly.

These word-finding errors occur with words whose pronunciation is very familiar to the speaker and have been produced correctly in other situations (Fromkin,

1973; Shallice & Butterworth, 1977). Some of these word-finding errors have been called "spoonerisms."

Even though the word is known, there is difficulty retrieving all the sounds, or the order of the sounds, that make up that word. Sounds may be added (e.g., "prilimary" for *primary*), omitted (e.g., "ambilent" for *ambivalent*), substituted (e.g., "asortize" for *amortize*), or exchanged (e.g., "Irasel" for *Israel*) when verbalizing the word (Fromkin, 1973; Levelt, 1989; Shallice & Butterworth, 1977). Although not always, "Twists of the Tongue" often occur on long words (words of three or more syllables) or in two-or three-word combinations (e.g., "Mig Bac" for *Big Mac*).

For Further Reading
The "Twist of the Tongue" word-finding error has been studied by many researchers. For more information about the characteristics of the "Twist of the Tongue" word-finding error, consult Butterworth (1980, 1981, 1989, 1993), Goodglass and Wingfield (1997), Levelt (1989, 1993), Meyer, (1993), and Shattuck-Hufnagel (1993).

"Twist of the Tongue" Examples

Following are additional examples of "Twists of the Tongue." Continue the informal evaluation of your own word-finding skills by putting an X in the That's Me box if the word-finding error is typical of you when you have difficulty finding a word that is two or more syllables in length.

Sound-Omission Error

In this conversation, the speaker made a "Twist of the Tongue" error by omitting two syllables of the target word, *cornucopia*.

Sound-Exchange Error

In this conversation, the speaker made a "Twist of the Tongue" error by exchanging the syllables of the target word, *millennium*.

Sound-Addition Error

In this conversation, the speaker made a "Twist of the Tongue" error by adding a syllable to the target name, *Subaru*.

Sound-Substitution Error

In this conversation, the speaker made a "Twist of the Tongue" error by substituting the initial sound of the target word, *listener*.

Continue to think about your own word-finding skills as you read the following examples. If you have ever produced a "Twist of the Tongue" word-finding error similar to the example, enter an X in the That's Me column. Many X's in this column suggest that you have produced "Twist of the Tongue" word-finding errors when you failed to retrieve a word or name.

Target Word	"Twist of the Tongue" Examples	That's Me
Barkowski	"Mr. Barkski...will be late for the meeting."	◯
Furosemide	"I am taking...Furmid...daily."	◯
Ethiopia	"We need to know the history of Eopia."	◯
chocolate chip cookies	"I am going to buy a dozen cocalate chip chookies."	◯
peanut butter	"I like beanut putter and jelly sandwiches."	◯
ultimatum	"They gave her an ultinum."	◯
synergy	"The syngery is obvious."	◯

PART 2

Self-Evaluation and Word-Finding Strategies

Self-Evaluation of Your Word-Finding Skills

This chapter presents a Word-Finding Questionnaire to help you self-evaluate your word-finding skills. Following the questionnaire, word-finding characteristics are matched with the three types of word-finding errors discussed in Chapter 2.

The self-evaluation in this chapter will help you to identify the type of word-finding errors you experience most frequently. The following questions are addressed in this chapter.

- What types of word finding patterns do you demonstrate?
- What patterns are most common for each of the error types?
- What types of word finding errors do you make?

Identifying Your Word-Finding Patterns

The purpose of this Word-Finding Questionnaire is to guide you through a self-evaluation of your word-finding skills. Each question represents a behavioral characteristic of a type of word-finding error. As you read each question, think about your word-finding skills when you are speaking. Decide which behaviors listed are characteristic of your speaking patterns when you experience a word-finding difficulty. After you reflect on your word-finding skills indicate (check) whether you rarely, occasionally, or frequently demonstrate that behavior when you are speaking.

Word-Finding Questionnaire

The purpose of this questionnaire is to help you evaluate your word-finding skills. Read each question and indicate (check) whether you rarely, occasionally, or frequently display that behavioral characteristic when you are speaking.

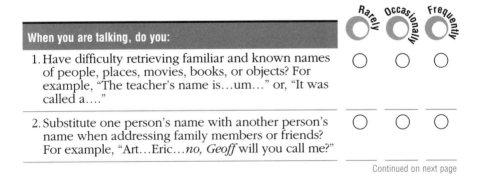

When you are talking, do you:	Rarely	Occasionally	Frequently
1. Have difficulty retrieving familiar and known names of people, places, movies, books, or objects? For example, "The teacher's name is...um..." or, "It was called a...."	O	O	O
2. Substitute one person's name with another person's name when addressing family members or friends? For example, "Art...Eric...*no, Geoff* will you call me?"	O	O	O

Continued on next page

3. Incorrectly pronounce long words that you know and that you have said correctly in other situations? For example, "It is merious…mier…*no, mysterious* what happened." — ○ ○ ○

4. Substitute the function of a word that you cannot retrieve? For example, "Do you have a…uh…lifter (jack) in the car?" — ○ ○ ○

5. Omit sounds of long words that you know? For example, say "conciene" when you mean to say *conscientious*. — ○ ○ ○

6. Substitute a word that sounds like the word you are trying to retrieve? For example, "I heard a lecture on archeology (architecture)." — ○ ○ ○

7. Use gestures that mime the action associated with a noun or verb that you cannot retrieve? For example, gesture writing for the word *pen*. — ○ ○ ○

8. Quickly misspeak, substituting a word in the same category as the target word? For example, "I like mustard (ketchup) on my burger." — ○ ○ ○

9. Exchange sounds of target words (e.g., "lispstick" for *lipstick*) or add sounds to target words (e.g., "lip sticker" for *lipstick*)? — ○ ○ ○

10. For the target word, substitute a word that is often said with other words? For example, "We will meet at Lake Michigan, I mean Lake Tahoe." — ○ ○ ○

11. Have a long delay before you retrieve the word? For example, "They are called…oh…um…uh… gardenias." — ○ ○ ○

12. Substitute sounds of target words (e.g., "stethacoop" for *stethoscope*)? — ○ ○ ○

Most Common Patterns for Each Error Type

The three types of word-finding errors ("Slip," "Tip," and "Twist of the Tongue") along with the corresponding behaviors that are typical of each of these error types are presented in this section.

A "Slip of the Tongue" – Word Substitution

"Slips of the Tongue" refer to those occasions when one misspeaks and substitutes an interfering word for the target word. The interfering word may be related to the target word in meaning (e.g., "washer" for *dryer*) or in sound form (e.g., "posterity" for *prosperity*).

The following word-finding behaviors are characteristic of individuals who produce "Slips of the Tongue" when they are speaking.

Behaviors Characteristic of the "Slip of the Tongue" Error

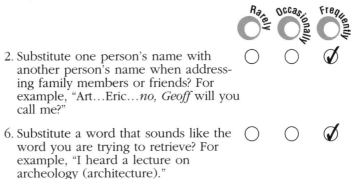

2. Substitute one person's name with another person's name when addressing family members or friends? For example, "Art...Eric...*no, Geoff* will you call me?"

6. Substitute a word that sounds like the word you are trying to retrieve? For example, "I heard a lecture on archeology (architecture)."

8. Quickly misspeak, substituting a word ○ ✓ ○
in the same category as the target word?
For example, "I like mustard (ketchup)
on my burger."

10. For the target word, substitute a word ○ ○ ✓
that is often said with other words?
For example, "We will meet at Lake
Michigan, I mean Lake Tahoe."

If you checked Occasionally or Frequently one or more times for items 2, 6, 8, and 10 on the Word-Finding Questionnaire you may be producing "Slips of the Tongue" when you are having difficulty finding words.

A "Tip of the Tongue" – Lost Word

The "Tip of Tongue" phenomenon occurs when the retrieval of a word is temporarily not possible, but is believed to be imminent. You have the word in mind, but you cannot say it. You may have a sense of the word's first sound or number of syllables.

The following word-finding behavioral characteristics are typical of individuals who have "Tip of the Tongue" experiences when talking.

Behaviors Characteristic of the "Tip of the Tongue" Experience

Rarely Occasionally Frequently

1. Have difficulty retrieving familiar and ○ ○ ✓
known names of people, places,
movies, books, or objects? For example,
"The teacher's name is…um…" or,
"It was called a…."

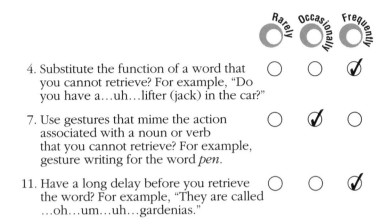

4. Substitute the function of a word that you cannot retrieve? For example, "Do you have a…uh…lifter (jack) in the car?"   ○ ○ ✓

7. Use gestures that mime the action associated with a noun or verb that you cannot retrieve? For example, gesture writing for the word *pen*.   ○ ✓ ○

11. Have a long delay before you retrieve the word? For example, "They are called …oh…um…uh…gardenias."   ○ ○ ✓

If you checked Occasionally or Frequently one or more times for items 1, 4, 7, and 11 on the Word-Finding Questionnaire, you may be having "Tip of the Tongue" experiences when you are having difficulty finding words.

A "Twist of the Tongue" – Word Attempt

"Twists of the Tongue" refer to those occasions when you omit or exchange sounds or syllables of long names or words that you know and have previously said correctly.

The following word-finding behaviors are characteristic of individuals who produce the "Twist of the Tongue" error.

Behaviors Characteristic of the "Twist of the Tongue" Error

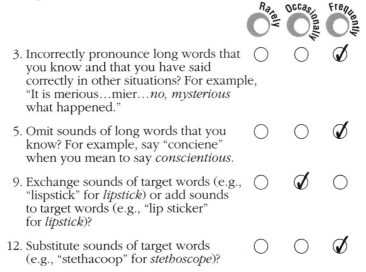

	Rarely	Occasionally	Frequently
3. Incorrectly pronounce long words that you know and that you have said correctly in other situations? For example, "It is merious...mier...*no, mysterious* what happened."	○	○	✓
5. Omit sounds of long words that you know? For example, say "conciene" when you mean to say *conscientious*.	○	○	✓
9. Exchange sounds of target words (e.g., "lipstick" for *lipstick*) or add sounds to target words (e.g., "lip sticker" for *lipstick*)?	○	✓	○
12. Substitute sounds of target words (e.g., "stethacoop" for *stethoscope*)?	○	○	✓

If you checked Occasionally or Frequently one or more times for items 3, 5, 9, and 12, on the Word-Finding Questionnaire, you may be making "Twists of the Tongue" errors when you are having difficulty finding words.

A "Slip," "Tip," and "Twist of the Tongue"

Often individuals produce all three of the word-finding error types discussed in this chapter. If you find that you exhibit "Slips," "Tips," and "Twists of the Tongue" when you are talking, study and use all the strategies presented in Chapter 4 to reduce the occurrence of these word-finding errors.

Strategies Are the Key

This chapter describes many useful word-finding strategies. The following questions are addressed.

- What are word-finding strategies?
- What are the specific word-finding strategies?
- What are the steps in applying each of these strategies?
- When would you use these word-finding strategies?
- When would you *not* use these word-finding strategies?

What Are Word-Finding Strategies?

Word-finding strategies are memory tactics that aid retrieval of specific target words and can help you improve your word-finding skills. Word-finding strategies are used before speaking as well as while one is speaking.

Specific Word-Finding Strategies

There are six categories of word-finding strategies presented in this book. Each has a different focus. The first group of strategies is called *Association Cueing Strategies* (German, 1993). Based on our understanding of memory processes (Higbee, 1993), these strategies direct you to associate, or link, elusive target words to words that are more readily accessible. The Association Cueing Strategies include the

- Same-Sounds Cue,
- Same-Sounds Meaning Cue, and
- Familiar-Word Cue.

Note: The Association Cueing Strategies presented in this book differ from those memory strategies that direct you to associate an idea (e.g., "Christmas flower" for *poinsettia*), or an image (e.g., "red flower" for *poinsettia*) to a new name or word. Those memory strategies are focused on helping you to remember the concepts associated with words and names that you are in the process of *learning*. In contrast, the

Association Cueing Strategies presented in this book focus on helping you retrieve the sound form of target words that you already *know*.

The second group of strategies is referred to as *Syllable-Dividing Strategies* (German, 1993). These strategies direct you to analyze the target word itself. They include

- Visual Syllable-Dividing and
- Rhythm Syllable-Dividing.

The third group of strategies is referred to as *Alternate Word Strategies* (German, 1993; Harrell, Parenté, Bellingrath, & Lisicia, 1992). These strategies direct you to select an alternate word to circumvent a word-finding block. They include

- Synonym Substituting and
- Category-Name Substituting.

The fourth strategy is *Pausing* (German, 1993; Harrell, Parenté, Bellingrath, & Lisicia, 1992). This strategy directs you to slow down the speaking process.

The fifth strategy, *Self-Correction*, is designed to help you self-monitor and self-correct your word-finding errors.

Finally, the sixth strategy, a practicing strategy called *Rehearsal*, is used with the first five word-finding strategies (Conca, 1989; German, 1993; Lesser, 1989; Parenté & Herrmann, 1996). The following are descriptions of each of these word-finding strategies. Figure 4.1 illustrates these various strategies.

Figure 4.1. Six Categories of Word-Finding Strategies

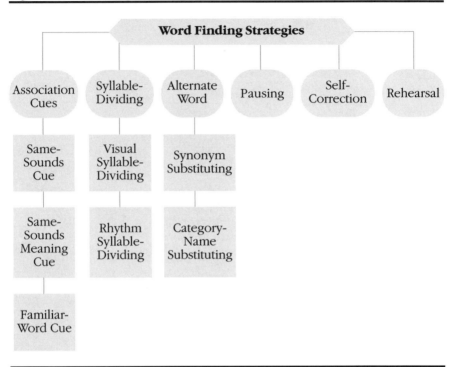

Association Cue Strategies

Association cues are "prompts" you use to help you find words while you are talking. When you use an association cue you associate, or link, a prompt word with the word you want to retrieve (the target word). You select the cue and practice using it before the speaking situation. Then you think of the cue while you are talking to help you retrieve the target word.

There are three types of Association Cues discussed in this section.

- Same-Sounds Cue
- Same-Sounds Meaning Cue
- Familiar-Word Cue

Same-Sounds Cue

The Same-Sounds Cue is a prompt word that shares some of the same sounds as the target word. When using this strategy to improve your word-finding skills, you associate or link to the target word, a prompt word that sounds like the word you want to retrieve (e.g., pointer for poinsettia). The Same-Sounds Cue focuses on helping you retrieve the sounds of the target word. The Rehearsal Strategy, described later in this chapter, is always used with a Same-Sounds Cue.

Steps to Apply the Same-Sounds Cue Strategy

1. Identify the target name or word (e.g., *tulip*).

2. Associate the target name or word with a prompt word or phrase that sounds like the target name or word (e.g., *tool*).

3. Review this link between the Same-Sounds Cue and the target word by thinking of the prompt word (do not say the prompt word aloud) while saying the target name or word out loud—(…tool) **"Tulip."**

4. Rehearse application of this strategy by thinking of the Same-Sounds Cue (do not say aloud) while saying the target name or word out loud in a sentence—(…tool) **"Tulip is a spring flower."**

5. Rehearse application of this strategy in three sentences or until you feel that you have overpracticed the target name or word and will consistently retrieve it.

a) (…tool) **"Tulips are a favorite of the deer."**

b) (…tool) "_____"
(Write your own sentence here and rehearse it out loud.)

c) (…tool) "_____"
(Write your own sentence here and rehearse it out loud.)

 ### *When to Use the Same-Sounds Cue Strategy*

This strategy can help you improve your word finding for those known words or names whose sounds you are not able to remember. Apply this strategy after you have had a "Tip of the Tongue" experience with a target word that can easily be matched with a Same-Sounds Cue. Also use this strategy with multisyllabic words to reduce twists of the tongue. Practice this strategy when you are alone prior to the next situation when you may be saying these names or words. (*Note:* Two good sources for identifying Same-Sounds Cues for target words are the dictionary and electronic word lists available on-line.) Figure 4.2 indicates the word-finding strategies appropriate for each of the word-finding error types.

 ### Same-Sounds Meaning Cue

Same-Sounds Meaning Cue is a prompt word(s) that shares some of the same sounds as the target word and is linked to the target word in meaning. When

Figure 4.2. Word-Finding Strategies for Each Word-Finding Error Type

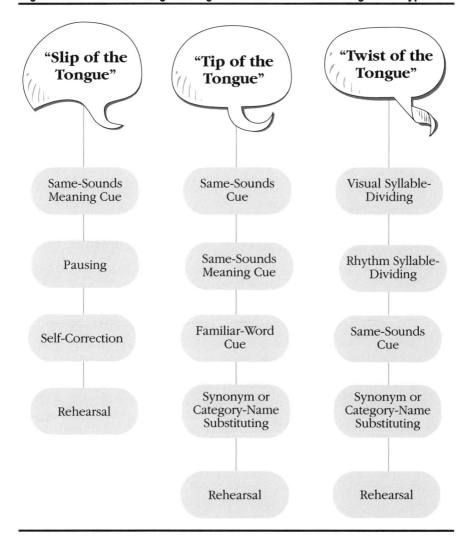

"Slip of the Tongue"	"Tip of the Tongue"	"Twist of the Tongue"
Same-Sounds Meaning Cue	Same-Sounds Cue	Visual Syllable-Dividing
Pausing	Same-Sounds Meaning Cue	Rhythm Syllable-Dividing
Self-Correction	Familiar-Word Cue	Same-Sounds Cue
Rehearsal	Synonym or Category-Name Substituting	Synonym or Category-Name Substituting
	Rehearsal	Rehearsal

using this strategy to improve your word-finding skills
you associate, or link, a prompt word(s) that both
sounds like the target name and is related to the target

name in meaning (e.g., gym for Jim, who is an athlete). The Rehearsal Strategy is always used with a Same-Sounds Meaning Cue.

Steps to Apply the Same-Sounds Meaning Cue Strategy

1. Identify the target name or word (e.g., Jim).

2. Associate the target name or word with a prompt word or phrase that both sounds like and is related in meaning to the target name or word (e.g., *gym*).

3. Review this link between the Same-Sounds Meaning Cue and the target word by thinking of the prompt word(s) (do not say the prompt aloud) while saying the target word out loud—(...gym) **"Jim."**

4. Rehearse application of this strategy by thinking of the Same-Sounds Meaning Cue (do not say aloud) while saying the target name or word aloud in a sentence—(...gym) **"Jim works out two hours a day."**

5. Rehearse application of this strategy in three sentences or until you feel that you have overpracticed the target name or word and will retrieve it consistently.

   a) (...gym) **"Jim runs an eight minute mile."**

   b) (...gym) "_____"

   (Write your own sentence here and rehearse it out loud.)

   c) (...gym) "_____"

   (Write your own sentence here and rehearse it out loud.)

When to Use the Same-Sounds Meaning Cue Strategy

Use the Same-Sounds Meaning Cue with personal names and names of places and things to reduce "Slips of the Tongue" and "Tips of the Tongue" with those names. Use this strategy with target words that you can easily match with Same-Sounds and Same-Sounds Meaning Cues. Practice this strategy when you are alone prior to the situation when you may be saying those names or words (see Figure 4.2).

Familiar-Word Cue

A Familiar-Word Cue is a cue word(s) that has been said frequently with the target name or word in other contexts. When using this strategy to improve your word-finding skills you associate, or link, this Familiar-Word Cue to the target word (e.g., Barbie doll for the name Barbie).The Rehearsal Strategy is always used with the Familiar-Word Cue.

Steps to Apply the Familiar-Word Cue Strategy

1. Identify the target name or word (e.g., Barbie).

2. Associate, or link, the target name or word with a prompt word or phrase that has been said with the target name or word in other contexts (e.g., Barbie doll).

3. Review this link between the Familiar-Word Cue and the target word by thinking of the prompt word(s) (do not say the prompt aloud) while saying the target word out loud—(…Barbie doll) **"Barbie."**

4. Rehearse application of this strategy by thinking of the Familiar-Word Cue (do not say aloud) while saying the target name or word out loud in a sentence—(…Barbie doll) **"Barbie is an excellent leader."**

5. Rehearse application of the strategy in three sentences or until you feel that you have overpracticed the target name or word and will retrieve it consistently.

   a) (…Barbie doll) **"Barbie is going to be the next president of this organization."**

   b) (…Barbie doll) "_____"

   (Write your own sentence here and rehearse it out loud.)

   c) (…Barbie doll) "_____"

   (Write your own sentence here and rehearse it out loud.)

When to Use the Familiar-Word Cue Strategy

Use this strategy when you have a "Tip of the Tongue" experience. This strategy can help you improve your word finding for known words or names whose sound form you are not able to retrieve. Use this strategy with target words that may be difficult to match with a Same-Sounds Cue. Apply this strategy when your are alone prior to the situation when you may be saying those names or words (see Figure 4.2).

Syllable-Dividing Strategies

Syllable-Dividing Strategies focus on the problematic word, directing you to analyze the target word. These strategies are used before the speaking situation to help speakers retrieve long words. There are two types of Syllable-Dividing Strategies presented in this section

- Visual Syllable-Dividing and
- Rhythm Syllable-Dividing.

Visual Syllable-Dividing

When using the Visual Syllable-Dividing Strategy to improve your word-finding skills, you divide the target word into syllables by writing the word on a piece of paper and drawing a line between each syllable (e.g., an / tith / e / sis). You then rehearse the target word by saying each syllable and then saying the word as a unit.

Steps to Apply the Visual Syllable-Dividing Strategy

1. Identify and write the target name or word (e.g., Beth-Halachmy).

2. Draw a line between each syllable (e.g., Beth / Ha / lach / my).

3. Rehearse the target name or word by saying each syllable out loud—**"Beth / Ha / lach / my."**

4. Rehearse the word as a unit three times or until you can say it automatically without hesitation—**"Beth-Halachmy, Beth-Halachmy, Beth-Halachmy."**

5. Rehearse the target word in three sentences or until you feel that you have overpracticed the pronunciation and will consistently retrieve it accurately.

   a) **"Beth-Halachmy is her last name."**

   b) "_____"

      (Write your own sentence here and rehearse it out loud.)

   c) "_____"

      (Write your own sentence here and rehearse it out loud.)

Rhythm Syllable-Dividing

When using the Rhythm Syllable-Dividing Strategy to improve your word-finding skills, you divide the target word into syllables by marking each syllable with a rhythmic tap for emphasis (e.g., *an ti the ses*). You then rehearse the target word by saying each syllable and then saying the word as a unit.

Steps to Apply the Rhythm Syllable-Dividing Strategy

1. Identify the target word (e.g., *immunology*).

2. As you say the target word, mark each syllable with a rhythmic tap to emphasize the syllables (e.g.,
   "im   mu   nol   o   gy").
     ∧   ∧   ∧   ∧   ∧

3. Rehearse the target word by saying each syllable with a tap—**"Im   mu   nol   o   gy."**
       ∧   ∧   ∧   ∧   ∧

4. Rehearse the word as a unit three times or until you can say it automatically without hesitation— **"Immunology, immunology, immunology."**

5. Rehearse the target word in three sentences or until you feel that you have overpracticed the pronunciation and will retrieve it consistently.

   a) **"Immunology is the medical study of your immune system."**

   b) "_____"

   (Write your own sentence here and rehearse it out loud.)

   c) "_____"

   (Write your own sentence here and rehearse it out loud.)

When to Use the Syllable-Dividing Strategies

Use the Syllable-Dividing Strategies to reduce "Twists of the Tongue" on known names or words that are three or more syllables in length. These would be words or names that you have said incorrectly producing a substitution that contained only some of the sounds of the target word. These strategies are always practiced before the speaking situation (see Figure 4.2).

Alternate Word Strategy

The Alternate Word Strategy is used while talking. This strategy directs speakers to substitute an alternate word for the target word that they are unable to retrieve. There are two types of Alternate Word Strategies presented in this section

- Synonym Substituting and
- Category-Name Substituting.

Synonym or Category-Name Substituting

When using this strategy, you think ahead while talking to identify the word which might cause you difficulty and then you substitute an alternate word(s) that is either similar in meaning (e.g., friendly for cordial) or names the category of the elusive word (e.g., vegetable for artichoke). The Rehearsal Strategy is always used with the Alternate Word Strategy.

Steps to Apply the Synonym or Category-Name Substituting Strategy

1. While you are talking, identify the elusive word that you anticipate having difficulty retrieving (e.g., *immense*).

2. Think of the category name or another word(s) that is similar in meaning to the elusive target word (e.g., *huge*).

3. Substitute the alternate word for the elusive word or name while you are talking—**"Their house is...huge."**

4. Rehearse application of this strategy prior to an event by thinking of alternative words, synonyms, or category names for target words or names that you think you might have difficulty retrieving in a conversation.

When to Use the Synonym or Category-Name Substituting Strategy

Use this strategy when you are talking and think you might have a "Tip of the Tongue" or "Twist of the Tongue" experience. Substitute alternate words for known words that you are not able to retrieve. Although you practice saying synonyms or category names for target words prior to the speaking situation, you use this strategy while you are talking (see Figure 4.2).

Pausing Strategy

The Pausing Strategy is used while you are talking. It is a strategy of slowing down used to inhibit the erroneous retrieval of a word that is interfering with the target word for selection. Use the Pausing Strategy strategically placed in the sentence. You purposefully pause before the noun or personal name in the sentence to avoid verbalizing the interfering word. This pausing procedure provides you with the time necessary to screen out the interfering word and select the target word.

Steps to Apply the Pausing Strategy

Apply this strategy during the course of conversation.

1. While you are speaking, pause immediately before the target name or word for which you believe there is an interfering word.
2. Screen out the interfering word and think of the target name or word—(...~~Rose~~, Rochelle) **"Rochelle."**

3. Continue the conversation saying the target name or word in the sentence—(...~~Rose~~, Rochelle) **"Rochelle will be here at 6:00."**

Rehearse application of this strategy prior to an event.

1. Identify the target name.
2. Rehearse saying the target name three times aloud. As you practice saying the target name, screen out the interfering name. Rehearse the target name silently and then say the target name out loud.
3. Rehearse saying aloud three sentences containing the target name. As you practice saying the target name in a sentence (a) pause immediately before the target name, (b) screen out the interfering name, (c) rehearse the target name silently, and then (d) say the sentence out loud with the target name.

When to Use the Pausing Strategy
Although you could practice using the Pausing Strategy when you are alone, you would utilize this strategy while you are talking to reduce "Slips of the Tongue" with names and words (see Figure 4.2).

Self-Correction Strategy

The Self-Correction Strategy is used to correct your word-finding errors while you are talking. It is a self-monitoring strategy whereby you listen to yourself as you are speaking. If you make a word-finding error, you correct the error before continuing your sentence.

Steps to Apply the Self-Correction Strategy

While you are speaking, pause immediately after you make a word-finding error and either:

A. say the correct target word (e.g., "The building is on Colfax, Michigan Street") or,

B. self-correct your word-finding error (e.g., "The building is on Colfax, no, I mean Michigan Street").

When to Self-Correct

If you find that listeners often remind you that you have made a word-finding error, you may not be aware of your "Slips of the Tongue." To become more aware of your word-finding errors, listen to and monitor your speech so that you can self-correct. Because a word-finding error can give a listener the impression that you do not know a word or name, it is always better to self-correct your word-finding errors. The self-correction informs the listener that you do know the target word and prevents you from presenting the wrong information (see Figure 4.2).

Rehearsal Strategy

The Rehearsal Strategy involves saying the target word aloud in isolation and in three sentences. Remember to always rehearse **out loud**. Rehearsing silently will not improve your word-finding skills when you are talking. Further, when using the Rehearsal Strategy with the Association Cueing Strategies, do not say the chosen cue out loud. Think of the association cue and only say the target name out loud. If you say or rehearse the association cue out loud you run the risk of retrieving the cue in place of the target word later when you are talking. For example, one individual used the Familiar Word Cue, *green bean*, to ensure retrieval of a keynote speaker's name, Mr. Green. Unfortunately he rehearsed both green bean and Mr. Green out loud several times prior to the meeting. Guess what happened when he introduced Mr. Green. Yes! He said, "We are pleased tonight to have Mr. Green Bean as out guest speaker."

Steps to Apply the Rehearsal Strategy

1. Identify the target names or words.

2. Rehearse the target name or word three times aloud. If you selected an association cue, think of (but do not say) the prompt word before you say the target word aloud.

3. Rehearse aloud three sentences containing the target word.

When to Use the Rehearsal Strategy

The Rehearsal Strategy is used with all the word-finding strategies and is always applied before the speaking situation (see Figure 4.2).

When *Not* to Use These Word-Finding Strategies

The purpose of this book is to provide you with retrieval strategies to improve your word-finding skills with names and words that you know. The word-finding strategies in this book do not teach you the meanings or concepts of words. Therefore, it would not be appropriate to apply these strategies to words or names that you do not know or that are not familiar to you. You should first learn the meanings of words before you apply word-finding strategies to anchor retrieval of those words.

In addition to retrieval strategies, both background knowledge and basic linguistic skill are required for the successful acquisition and use of vocabulary. These prerequisites for good retrieval are not provided by the retrieval strategies. Thus, an individual will also want to possess these language competencies to support successful application of the word-finding strategies presented in this book.

For Further Reading

The strategies presented in this chapter are only focused on the retrieval processes involved in saying words and do not address the entire scope of vocabulary acquisition or usage. Consult Bloom (1994); Coady and Huckin (1997); McKeown and Curtis (1987); and Pinker, (1995) for a fuller account of vocabulary acquisition and usage.

PART 3

The "Slip of the Tongue" Word-Finding Error

Getting Started

You were telling your neighbor that you enjoy seeing the forsythia bloom each spring. In sharing your excitement about the flower, you produced a "Slip of the Tongue" and said the name of another flower, *iris*.

I love it when the irises bloom.

A common word-finding difficulty is the interchanging of names or words. When this happens, an interfering word is verbalized rather than the name or word you intended to say. Speakers may interchange the names of family members, friends or coworkers. They may substitute wrong names for places and locations or they may exchange common nouns when they are talking. For example, parents call their children or grandchildren by their siblings' names. Other individuals interchange the names of friends. Still others may misspeak and exchange names of cities they visited, events they have attended, or things they have bought. These substitutions are examples of "Slips of the Tongue."

This chapter presents a list of things to do that will help you successfully handle those situations when you make a "Slip of the Tongue" word-finding error as well as aid you in reducing future difficulties with word finding. Following the steps in this list will help you present your ideas more fluently and be at your personal best when you are speaking.

1. Slow the pace of your speech.

2. Avoid ignoring "Slips of the Tongue" as it may result in you presenting inaccurate information.

3. Listen to yourself while you are talking so you can identify and self-correct your "Slips of the Tongue."

4. If you self-correct a word-finding error, continue talking after your self-correction to maintain a fluent conversation.

5. Avoid behaviors that will call attention to your errors, like shaking your head or grimacing when you make a "Slip of the Tongue" word-finding error.

6. Use the strategies presented in Chapter 6 to help reduce your "Slips of the Tongue."

Strategies to Reduce "Slips of the Tongue" with Names and Common Words

Alex...
Eric is coming
to dinner.

You were telling your spouse to expect your nephew for dinner. In relating the message you misspoke and said the name of your youngest nephew, Alex, in place of the name of your oldest nephew, Eric. The Pausing Strategy can help you stop or inhibit saying the incorrect name.

Substituting or interchanging names and words is an example of a "Slip of the Tongue" word-finding error. A slip of the tongue occurs when you verbalize an interfering word in place of the word you wanted to say. These interfering words are usually names or words that are

- of individuals who share the same relation to the speaker (e.g., Alex for Eric—both nephews),

- said in the same context as the target word (e.g., birthday candles for birthday cake),

- in the same category as the target word (e.g., mustard for ketchup or January for March), or

- similar in sound to the target word (e.g., emergency for emerging).

This chapter presents examples of how to apply word-finding strategies that can reduce slips of the tongue when saying proper names, names of places and things, and common words. First, strategies recommended to reduce slips of the tongue with names and words are reviewed. These include the Pausing Strategy, Same-Sounds Meaning Cue Strategy, and the Self-Correction Strategy. Second, examples of how to apply each of these strategies are presented. Third, practice charts are provided to help you automatically apply these strategies to names and words with which you have made slips of the tongue. Figure 6.1 displays the word-finding strategies recommended to reduce the "Slip of the Tongue" word-finding error.

Pausing Strategy

When using the Pausing Strategy, you pause, screen out the interfering name(s), and then verbalize the target name.

Same-Sounds Meaning Cue Strategy

When using the Same-Sounds Meaning Cue strategy, you link a prompt word with the target name or word

Figure 6.1. Word-Finding Strategies for the "Slip of the Tongue" Error

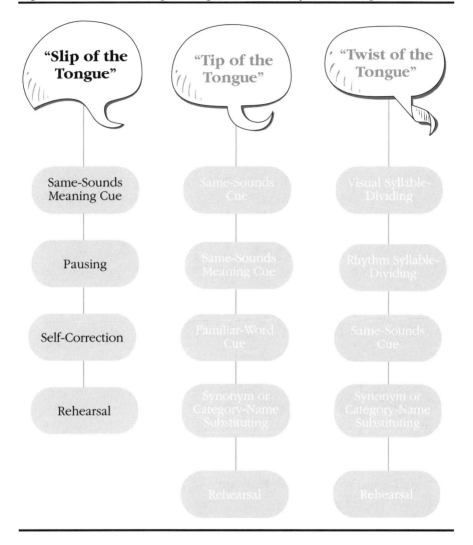

that both sounds like the target name or word and is linked to it in meaning.

Self-Correction Strategy

The Self-Correction Strategy is used to correct your word-finding errors while you are talking. As you listen to yourself, you identify your slips of the tongue and self-correct these errors before continuing your sentence.

Rehearsal Strategy

The Rehearsal Strategy involves rehearsing the target word by saying it aloud in isolation and in three sentences. *Do not say* the chosen cue out loud. Think of the cue and then say the target name or word aloud. Remember to always rehearse **out loud**. Rehearsing silently will not improve your word-finding skills when you are talking. Because the Rehearsal Strategy is used with all the word-finding strategies presented, application of this strategy is indicated with each of the word-finding strategies.

Using the Pausing Strategy with Proper Names

The Pausing Strategy helps reduce the verbalization of interfering names when addressing or referring to family members, friends, or coworkers. The interfering personal names are often names of individuals who (a) share a similar relationship with you (e.g., Mary for Diane—both friends or Eric for Alex—both nephews); or (b) sound similar to the target name (e.g., Pam for Ann). An important aspect of the Pausing Strategy is to apply it strategically. You insert the pause in your sentence immediately before the name you predict you will have difficulty retrieving (saying). Although you use the Pausing Strategy when speaking, practicing this strategy when you are alone will help you apply it automatically when addressing your children, grandchildren, or other family members.

> *Cindy (when you mean Ann) I need to talk to you.*

Let's assume that Mary's children are named Cindy and Ann. She often interchanges their names when addressing them. That is, when she wants to say Ann, Cindy's name interferes and she says Cindy instead of Ann.

To prevent verbalization of interfering names, use the Pausing Strategy. In this situation, Mary would pause, screen out the name Cindy and then say Ann's name out loud in the sentence. Apply the Pausing Strategy to inhibit saying interfering names when addressing family members by using the following steps.

Strategy Steps	Example
1. Identify the target name.	Target Name = Ann
2. Rehearse the Pausing Strategy with the target name.	As you prepare to say Ann, follow these steps. 1. Pause. 2. Screen out the interfering name, Cindy. 3. Rehearse the target name, Ann, silently. 4. Say Ann out loud. (… ~~Cindy~~, Ann) **"Ann"**

Continued on next page

Strategy Steps	Example
3. Rehearse the Pausing Strategy in three sentences.	1. (… ~~Cindy~~, Ann) **"Ann is my oldest daughter."** 2. (… ~~Cindy~~, Ann) **"Ann has two children."** 3. (… ~~Cindy~~, Ann) **"Ann is an accountant."**
4. Identify the target name.	Target Name = Cindy
5. Rehearse the Pausing Strategy with the target name.	As you prepare to say Cindy, follow these steps. 1. Pause. 2. Screen out the interfering name, Ann. 3. Rehearse the target name, Cindy, silently. 4. Say Cindy out loud. (…~~Ann~~, Cindy) **"Cindy"**
6. Rehearse the Pausing Strategy in three sentences.	1. (…~~Ann~~, Cindy) **"Cindy is my youngest daughter."** 2. (…~~Ann~~, Cindy) **"Cindy has a little boy."** 3. (…~~Ann~~, Cindy) **"Cindy is a corporate executive."**

Joe is a fantastic putter.

Let's assume that your golf partners are Joe and Geoff and you often interchange their names when you are talking about their golf game. That is, when you want to say Geoff's name, Joe's name intrudes and you say, "Joe is a fantastic putter."

Apply the Pausing Strategy in this situation to inhibit verbalization of the interfering name. Use the following steps to practice inhibiting interfering names when referring to individuals you know.

Strategy Steps	Example
1. Identify the target name.	Target Name = Geoff
2. Rehearse the Pausing Strategy with the target name.	As you prepare to say Geoff, follow these steps. 1. Pause. 2. Screen out the interfering name, Joe. 3. Rehearse the target name, Geoff, silently. 4. Say Geoff out loud. (...~~Joe~~, Geoff) **"Geoff"**
3. Rehearse the Pausing Strategy in three sentences.	1. (...~~Joe~~, Geoff) **"Geoff is a great golfer."** 2. (...~~Joe~~, Geoff) **"Geoff and I play on Mondays."** 3. (...~~Joe~~, Geoff) **"Geoff and I enjoy playing golf."**
4. Identify the target name.	Target Name = Joe
5. Rehearse the Pausing Strategy with the target name.	As you prepare to say Joe, follow these steps. 1. Pause. 2. Screen out the interfering name, Geoff. 3. Rehearse the target name, Joe, silently. 4. Say Joe out loud. (... ~~Geoff~~, Joe) **"Joe"**
6. Rehearse the Pausing Strategy in three sentences.	1. (... ~~Geoff~~, Joe) **"Joe is my uncle."** 2. (... ~~Geoff~~, Joe) **"Joe has a new set of clubs."** 3. (... ~~Geoff~~, Joe) **"Joe is a great putter."**

Practice Chart for Applying the Pausing Strategy

Select two proper names that you typically exchange when you are talking causing a "Slip of the Tongue" word-finding error. For initial practice only, apply the Pausing Strategy to those names by completing the following chart.

Strategy Steps	Fill In the Blanks
1. Identify the target name.	Target Name = _____
2. Rehearse the Pausing Strategy with the target name.	As you prepare to say _____ (target name), follow these steps. 1. Pause. 2. Screen out the interfering name, _____. 3. Rehearse the target name, _____, silently. 4. Say _____ (target name) out loud.
3. Write three sentences with the target name. Rehearse applying the Pausing Strategy in these sentences.	1. _____ 2. _____ 3. _____
4. Identify the target name.	Target Name = _____
5. Rehearse the Pausing Strategy with the target name.	As you prepare to say _____ (target name), follow these steps. 1. Pause. 2. Screen out the interfering name, _____. 3. Rehearse the target name, _____, silently. 4. Say _____ (target name) out loud.
6. Write three sentences with the target name. Rehearse applying the Pausing Strategy in these sentences.	1. _____ 2. _____ 3. _____

Using the Same-Sounds Meaning Cue with Proper Names

Some name groups or name pairs are particularly troublesome and result in "Slips of the Tongue" even when the Pausing Strategy is applied. In these situations it is also necessary to anchor the retrieval of these names with the Same-Sounds Meaning Cue Strategy. For example, a Same-Sounds Meaning Cue to aid retrieval of the name Ann might be *anise*. Anise is a Same-Sounds Cue because the target name, Ann, and the cue anise, share the same sounds (not spelling) in the first syllable. Anise would also be a Meaning Cue for the name Ann because Mary knows Ann loves the anise flavor.

Similarly, a Same-Sounds Meaning Cue to aid retrieval of the name Cindy might be Cinderella. Cinderella is a Same-Sounds Cue because the target name, Cindy, and the cue, Cinderella, share the same sounds (not spelling) in the first syllable. Cinderella is also a Meaning Cue for the name Cindy because Mary knows it is important to Cindy that everything be clean and neat. Apply the Same-Sounds Meaning Cue Strategy to anchor retrieval of interfering names by using the following steps.

Strategy Steps	Example
1. Identify the target names.	Target Names = Ann and Cindy
2. Using the Same-Sounds Meaning Cue, associate the target name with a prompt word or phrase that both sounds like the target name and is linked in meaning to the target name.	*Same-Sounds Cue:* Link Ann to the word *anise* because the name and the word each begin with the same first sounds. *Meaning Cue:* Anise is also a meaning cue because Mary knows that Ann likes the anise flavor.

Continued on next page

Strategy Steps	Example
	Same-Sounds Cue: Link Cindy to the name *Cinderella* because each name begins with the same first sounds.
	Meaning Cue: Cinderella is also a meaning cue because Mary knows that it is important to Cindy to keep everything clean and neat.
3. Review this link between the Same-Sounds Meaning Cue and the target name by thinking of the prompt word immediately before saying the target name out loud.	Think of the cue *anise* immediately before saying Ann aloud. (…anise) **"Ann"** Think of the cue *Cinderella* immediately before saying Cindy aloud. (…Cinderella) **"Cindy"**
4. Rehearse application of this strategy in three sentences or until you feel that you have overpracticed the target name and will retrieve it consistently.	1. Think of the cue *anise* immediately before saying the target name aloud in the sentence. (…anise) **"Ann is my oldest daughter."** 2. Think of the cue *anise* immediately before saying the target name aloud in the sentence. (…anise) **"Ann is a good swimmer."** 3. Think of the cue *anise* immediately before saying the target name aloud in the sentence. (…anise) **"Ann has two children."**
5. Rehearse application of this strategy in three sentences or until you feel that you have overpracticed the target name and will retrieve it consistently.	1. Think of the cue *Cinderella* immediately before saying the target name aloud in the sentence. (…Cinderella) **"Cindy is my youngest daughter."** 2. Think of the cue *Cinderella* immediately before saying the target name aloud in the sentence. (…Cinderella) **"Cindy is very organized."** 3. Think of the cue *Cinderella* immediately before saying the target name aloud in the sentence. (…Cinderella) **"Cindy has a little boy."**

Practice Chart for Applying the Same-Sounds Meaning Cue Strategy

Use the two proper names you selected earlier and for initial practice only, apply the Same-Sounds Meaning Cue Strategy to these names by completing the following chart. Figure 6.2 illustrates the application of the Same-Sounds Meaning Cue Strategy.

Strategy Steps	Fill In the Blanks
1. Identify the target names.	Target Names = _____ and _____
2. Using the Same-Sounds Meaning Cue, associate the target name with a prompt word or phrase that both sounds like the target name and is linked in meaning to the target name.	*Same-Sounds Cue:* Link _____ (target name) to _____ (cue) because the target name and the cue word each begin with the same first sounds. *Meaning Cue:* _____ is also a meaning cue because _____. *Same-Sounds Cue:* Link _____ (target name) to _____ (cue) because the target name and the cue word each begin with the same first sounds. *Meaning Cue:* _____ is also a meaning cue because_____.
3. Review this link between the Same-Sounds Meaning Cue and the target name by thinking of the prompt word immediately before saying the target name out loud.	Think of _____ (cue) immediately before saying _____ (target name) aloud. Think of _____ (cue) immediately before saying _____ (target name) aloud.
4. Write three sentences with the first target name. Rehearse applying the Same-Sounds Meaning Cue Strategy in these sentences or until you feel that you have overpracticed the target name and will retrieve it consistently.	1. _____ 2. _____ 3. _____

Continued on next page

Strategy Steps	Fill In the Blanks
5. Write three sentences with the second target name. Rehearse applying the Same-Sounds Meaning Cue Strategy in these sentences or until you feel that you have overpracticed the target name and will retrieve it consistently.	1. _____ 2. _____ 3. _____

Figure 6.2. Using Word-Finding Strategies to Reduce "Slips of the Tongue" When Retrieving Personal Names

Word-Finding Error	Word-Finding Strategies	Application of Strategy	Rehearse Word-Finding Strategy in Three Sentences
Calling Cindy by Ann's name (substituting oldest daughter's name with youngest daughter's name)	**Same-Sounds Meaning Cue** Cinderella, same initial sounds as target name Cindy and Cinderella is associated with being neat.	Think of cue *Cinderella* silently before saying target name, **"Cindy"** out loud.	Pause, think of cue *Cinderella* before saying target name, **"Cindy"** out loud in three sentences. 1. (…Cinderella) **"Cindy is my youngest daughter."**
	Pausing Pause before saying target name.	Pause to screen out the interfering name, Ann, before saying, **"Cindy."**	2. (…Cinderella) **"Cindy has a little boy."** 3. (…Cinderella) **"Cindy is very organized."**

Examples of Applying Word-Finding Strategies to Reduce "Slips of the Tongue" with Names of Places, Events, and Entities

This is a great day for Notre Dame, Northwestern.

It was a special event for Northwestern University. However, the university spokesman misspoke when he announced to the crowd, "This is a great day for Notre Dame." He meant to say, "This is a great day for Northwestern."

Interchanging names of places and entities (e.g., names of localities, cities, institutions, companies, medicines, movies, or books) is a common word-finding difficulty. For example, in the preceding illustration the name Notre Dame interfered with the selection of the name Northwestern and was verbalized. Notre Dame and Northwestern are related in meaning because they are both names of universities and are related in form because they begin with the same sounds. Although these errors are commonly called "bloopers," they are "Slip of the Tongue" word-finding errors.

"Slips of the Tongue" can occur in many speaking situations. When referring to names of stores, individuals may substitute store names that provide the same service (e.g., Walgreens for Osco—both are pharmacies); when saying city names, speakers may substitute cities in the same state (e.g., South Bend for Valparaiso—both are cities in Indiana); or when referring to medicines speakers may substitute names of similar sounding medicines (e.g., Minocycline for

Methacycline). This section presents examples of how to apply the Pausing Strategy to reduce "Slips of the Tongue" when saying names of places, events, and entities.

Meet me at the gate for American flight 2980.

Let's assume that you are going to an out-of-town meeting with your supervisor. You intended to leave her a voice mail explaining that you have her tickets and will meet her at the gate to board United Airlines flight 2980. However, because you misspoke and told her to meet you at the American gate, she waited for you at the wrong terminal.

Next time you are leaving a voice mail, apply the Pausing Strategy to inhibit verbalization of any interfering names. Use the following steps to practice inhibiting interfering names when referring to names of places, events, or entities that you know.

Strategy Steps	Example
1. Identify the target name.	Target Name = United
2. Rehearse the Pausing Strategy with the target name.	As you prepare to say United, follow these steps. 1. Pause. 2. Screen out the interfering name, American. 3. Rehearse the target name, United, silently. 4. Say United out loud. (… ~~American~~, United) **"United"**
3. Rehearse the Pausing Strategy in three sentences.	1. (… ~~American~~, United) **"United flight 2980 will be on time."** 2. (… ~~American~~, United) **"United flight 2980 will leave from gate six."** 3. (… ~~American~~, United) **"United flight 2980 is full."**

Practice Chart for Applying the Pausing Strategy

Select two names of either places, events, or entities that you have typically exchanged when you were talking or that might cause a "Slip of the Tongue" word-finding error. For initial practice only, apply the Pausing Strategy to those names by completing the following chart.

Strategy Steps	Fill In the Blanks
1. Identify the target name.	Target Name = _____
2. Rehearse the Pausing Strategy with the target name.	As you prepare to say _____ (target name), follow these steps. 1. Pause. 2. Screen out the interfering name, _____. 3. Rehearse the target name, _____, silently. 4. Say _____ (target name) out loud.
3. Write three sentences with the target name. Rehearse applying the Pausing Strategy in these sentences.	1. _____ 2. _____ 3. _____

Continued on next page

Strategy Steps	Fill In the Blanks
4. Identify the target name.	Target Name = _____
5. Rehearse the Pausing Strategy with the target name.	As you prepare to say _____ (target name), follow these steps. 1. Pause. 2. Screen out the interfering name, _____. 3. Rehearse the target name, _____, silently. 4. Say _____ (target name) out loud.
6. Write three sentences with the target name. Rehearse applying the Pausing Strategy in these sentences.	1. _____ 2. _____ 3. _____

Examples of Applying Word-Finding Strategies to Reduce "Slips of the Tongue" with Common Words

I need fat-free bonds to diversify my portfolio.

Art was explaining to his accountant the type of investments he wanted to make for the coming year. The word *fat* interfered with his selection of the word *tax* because the words *fat* and *tax* frequently co-occur with the target word *free* (e.g., fat-free, tax-free). The Pausing Strategy can help Art screen out interfering words that may co-occur with other words in a sentence.

"Slips of the Tongue" with common nouns or verbs, adjectives, or adverbs occur frequently and often take special effort to inhibit. This section presents word-finding strategies that can help reduce these word-finding errors with common words.

I bid two hearts, I mean two diamonds.

Let's assume that you are an avid bridge player. In fact, you are pretty good, if you say so yourself. However, you find yourself mistakenly saying the wrong suits of the cards when bidding. You may say hearts instead of diamonds, or clubs instead of spades.

To stop the verbalization of interfering words that share meaning with the target word, use the Pausing Strategy the next time you are playing bridge. For example, deliberately pause until you have screened out hearts and rehearsed silently the correct card suit, diamonds. Then say the word out loud to bid. Although you will use the Pausing Strategy when playing bridge, practicing this strategy when you are alone will help you to apply it automatically when you are playing cards. Use the following steps to keep from saying the interfering word when speaking.

Strategy Steps	Example
1. Identify the target noun.	Target Noun = diamonds
2. Rehearse the Pausing Strategy with the target noun.	As you prepare to say diamonds, follow these steps. 1. Pause. 2. Screen out any interfering words (e.g., clubs, hearts, or spades). 3. Rehearse the target noun, *diamonds*, silently. 4. Say diamonds out loud. (… ~~hearts~~, diamonds) **"Diamonds"**
3. Rehearse the Pausing Strategy in three sentences.	1. (… ~~hearts~~, diamonds) **"Diamonds is my best bid."** 2. **"I will bid** (… ~~hearts~~, diamonds) **diamonds."** 3. **"My bid is** (… ~~hearts~~, diamonds) **diamonds."**

Did you turn on the disposal …I mean the dishwasher?

Let's assume you asked your spouse to turn on the dishwasher. In doing so, you said disposal as you searched for the word *dishwasher*.

To stop the verbalization of interfering words that are in the same category as the target word, use the Pausing Strategy the next time you are making a request. For example, deliberately pause until you have screened out interfering words in the same category as the target noun. Use the following steps to keep from saying interfering words when speaking.

Strategy Steps	Example
1. Identify the target noun.	Target Noun = dishwasher
2. Rehearse the Pausing Strategy with the target noun.	As you prepare to ask your spouse if he or she turned on the dishwasher, follow these steps. 1. Pause. 2. Screen out any interfering words (e.g., disposal). 3. Rehearse the target noun, *dishwasher*, silently. 4. Say dishwasher out loud. (... ~~disposal~~, dishwasher) **"Dishwasher"**
3. Rehearse the Pausing Strategy in three sentence.	1. **"Did you turn on the** (... ~~disposal~~ dishwasher) **dishwasher?"** 2. **"I turned on the** (... ~~disposal~~, dishwasher) **dishwasher."** 3. **"Please turn on the** (... ~~disposal~~, dishwasher) **dishwasher."**

Practice Chart for Applying the Pausing Strategy

Select two common words that you typically exchange when you are talking causing a "Slip of the Tongue" word-finding error. For initial practice only, apply the Pausing Strategy to these words by completing the following chart.

Strategy Steps	Fill In the Blanks
1. Identify the target word.	Target Word = _____
2. Rehearse the Pausing Strategy with the target word.	As you prepare to say _____ (target word), follow these steps. 1. Pause. 2. Screen out the interfering word, _____. 3. Rehearse the target word, _____, silently. 4. Say _____ (target word) out loud.
3. Write three sentences with the target word. Rehearse applying the Pausing Strategy in these sentences.	1. _____ 2. _____ 3. _____
4. Identify the target word.	Target Word = _____
5. Rehearse the Pausing Strategy with the target word.	As you prepare to say _____ (target word), follow these steps. 1. Pause. 2. Screen out the interfering word, _____. 3. Rehearse the target word, _____, silently. 4. Say _____ (target word) out loud.
6. Write three sentences with the target word. Rehearse applying the Pausing Strategy in these sentences.	1. _____ 2. _____ 3. _____

Using the Self-Correction Strategy

Please pick up potatoes, carrots, and celery at the store.

Let's assume that you left a voice mail for your partner asking him or her to pick up some items at the grocery store that you need for dinner that night. The list includes items whose names could easily be substituted. You asked your partner to pick up potatoes, carrots, and celery. You meant to ask for tomatoes, carrots, and celery. You substituted potatoes for tomatoes and did not self-correct. Consequently, your partner came home with potatoes instead of tomatoes.

This example demonstrates how important it is to self-monitor our speech and self-correct our word-finding errors to ensure accurate communication. If you had done so, your partner would have brought home tomatoes.

The Self-Correction Strategy will improve your communication when you make a word-finding error. To self-correct your "Slips of the Tongue," listen to yourself as you are talking and immediately after your word-finding error you either say, "I mean..." inserting the target word to correct your error or simply insert your correction before continuing your sentence. In this situation the speaker would say, "Please pick up potatoes, I mean tomatoes, carrots, and celery at the store."

Final Guidelines for Applying Strategies to Reduce "Slips of the Tongue"

This chapter presents final guidelines for applying strategies to reduce "Slips of the Tongue" with names and words you know. Following these guidelines, try each strategy in Chapter 6 to determine which ones are most appropriate for your word-finding style. Once you determine which strategies help you reduce your "Slips of the Tongue," use those strategies consistently to improve your retrieval of known names and words.

Final Guidelines

- Identify the specific name or word in a sentence that you think you might substitute.
- Apply the Pausing Strategy before you say this name or word to create time to inhibit interfering names or words.
- Establish Same-Sounds Meaning Cues for particularly troublesome pairs or groups of names or words.
- When you are alone, rehearse using the selected strategies in several sentences.
- Use the Self-Correction Strategy to self-monitor and self-correct your "Slips of the Tongue."

Once you have followed these guidelines and applied strategies to troublesome names and words, you should see improvement in saying those words accurately across speaking situations. However, if you find that you are still producing "Slips of the Tongue" when speaking, follow these guidelines to reapply and rehearse the strategies suggested for the "Slip of the Tongue" word-finding error.

PART 4

The "Tip of the Tongue" Word-Finding Error

Getting Started

I love it when the …um…um… they're yellow….

Rita is at a party talking with her neighbors. She has a "Tip of the Tongue" experience when she tells them how much she loves it when her forsythia bush blooms in the spring.

Many individuals report that they have difficulty remembering proper names; names of places, events, or entities; as well as remembering common words. Even though they know and have said the names or words before, they indicate that they momentarily forget the names or words just when they need to be said. They report that at times they feel as if the name or word is on the tip of their tongue.

This chapter presents a list of things to do that will help you successfully handle a "Tip of the Tongue" experience when talking as well as reduce future difficulties with word finding. Following the suggestions in this list will help you present your ideas more fluently and be at your personal best when you are speaking.

1. While speaking, think ahead to identify words that you may have difficulty retrieving.
   - If you have identified a potentially elusive word, switch to a synonym or category name for the target idea to keep from having a "Tip of the Tongue" experience.
   - When you remember the name or word, apply the word-finding strategies to avoid future "Tip of the Tongue" experiences with that name or word.
2. Refrain from saying, "I am always forgetting people's names" or, "I am having a senior moment." These behaviors call attention to your word-finding difficulty.
3. Avoid snapping your fingers or any other gestures that indicate frustration with your inability to remember a word or name. These behaviors distract from the message your are trying to convey.
4. Use the strategies presented in Chapter 9 to help reduce "Tip of the Tongue" experiences.

Strategies to Reduce "Tip of the Tongue" Errors with Names and Common Words

Kate, I would like you to meet...um....

Carol is at a party and she wants to introduce Kate to her coworker. However, she has a "Tip of the Tongue" experience when she momentarily forgets her coworker's name. The Association Cue Strategies can help Carol in future conversations when she has to retrieve an individual's name.

This chapter presents examples of how to apply word-finding strategies that can reduce tip of the tongue experiences when you are trying to retrieve names and words that you know. First, strategies recommended to reduce tip of the tongue experiences with names and words are reviewed. These include the Association Cue Strategies, the Alternate Word Strategy, and the Rehearsal Strategy. Second, examples of how to apply each of these strategies are presented. Third, practice charts are provided to help you automatically apply these strategies to names and words with which you have had a tip of the tongue experience. Figure 9.1 displays the word-finding strategies to help reduce "Tip of the Tongue" experiences.

Same-Sounds Cue Strategy

The Same-Sounds Cue Strategy directs the speaker to link the target word to a cue word that sounds like (shares similar sounds) the target word.

Same-Sounds Meaning Cue Strategy

The Same-Sounds Meaning Cue Strategy directs the speaker to link the target name with a word that both sounds like the target name or word and is linked to it in meaning.

Familiar-Word Cue Strategy

The Familiar-Word Cue directs the speaker to link the target word to a prompt word(s) that has frequently been said with the target word in other contexts.

Synonym or Category-Name Substituting Strategy

The Alternate Word Strategy directs you to substitute a synonym or category name for the elusive target word that you are unable to retrieve.

Figure 9.1. Word-Finding Strategies to Reduce the "Tip of the Tongue" Experience

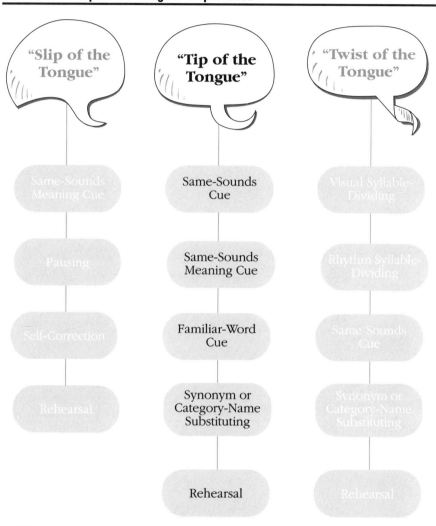

Rehearsal Strategy

The Rehearsal Strategy involves rehearsing the target word by saying it aloud in isolation and in three sentences. *Do not say* the chosen cue out loud. Think of the cue and then say the target name or word aloud. Remember to always rehearse **out loud**. Rehearsing silently will not improve your word-finding skills when you are talking. Because the Rehearsal Strategy is used with all the word-finding strategies presented, application of this strategy is indicated with each of the word-finding strategies.

Examples of Applying Word-Finding Strategies to Reduce "Tip of the Tongue" Experiences with Proper Names

I want you to meet Sandy's husband ...um...uh....

Let's assume that you are going to a party on Saturday night. You want to remember the names of your friends' spouses so that you can introduce them to your partner. You want to be sure to remember the names of Sandy's husband, Andrew; David's wife, Meryl; and Donna's husband, Phil.

Same-Sounds Meaning Cue Strategy

Personal names of family members and friends are often vulnerable to "Tip of the Tongue" experiences and are the most difficult to retrieve consistently. The Same-Sounds Meaning Cue Strategy is recommended to improve your retrieval of personal names that you know, but may momentarily forget. The following is an example of how to apply the Same-Sounds Meaning Cue Strategy to aid retrieval of someone's name. Follow the steps indicated to avoid having a "Tip of the Tongue" experience when you are introducing friends. *Note:* If the target name is not easily matched to a Same-Sounds Meaning Cue, apply a Same-Sounds Cue only or a Familiar-Word Cue.

Strategy Steps	Example
1. Identify the target names.	Target Names = Andrew, Meryl, and Phil
2. Using the Same-Sounds Meaning Cue, associate the target name with a prompt word or phrase that both sounds like the target name and is linked in meaning to the target name.	*Same-Sounds Cue:* Link Andrew to the phrase *Prince Andrew* because the name Andrew is repeated. *Meaning Cue:* Prince Andrew is also a meaning cue because Sandy has told you that she views Andrew as a leader. *Same-Sounds Cue:* Link Meryl with the actress *Meryl Streep* because the name Meryl is repeated. *Meaning Cue:* Meryl Streep is also a meaning cue because your friend Meryl performs in a local theater company. *Same-Sounds Cue:* Link Phil with the word *philharmonic* because Phil and philharmonic have the same sounds in the first syllable. *Meaning Cue:* Philharmonic is also a meaning cue because you know that Phil and Donna enjoy the symphony.

Continued on next page

Strategy Steps	Example

3. Review this link between the Same-Sounds Meaning Cue and the target name by thinking of the prompt word immediately before saying the target name out loud.	Think of the cue *Prince Andrew* immediately before saying Andrew aloud.
	    (...Prince Andrew) **"Andrew"**
	
	Think of the cue *Meryl Streep* immediately before saying Meryl aloud.
	    (...Meryl Streep) **"Meryl"**
	
	Think of the cue *philharmonic* immediately before saying Phil aloud.
	    (...philharmonic) **"Phil"**

4. Rehearse application of this strategy in three sentences or until you feel that you have overpracticed the target names and will retrieve them consistently.	Think of each cue immediately before saying the target name aloud in a sentence. 1. (...Prince Andrew) **"Andrew is Sandy's husband."** 2. (...Meryl Streep) **"Meryl is John's wife."** 3. (....philharmonic) **"Phil is Donna's husband."**

I would recommend you call...um...uh...he is great.

Let's assume that you were recommending an instructor, named Jim, to a colleague. You momentarily have a "Tip of the Tongue" experience and cannot retrieve the instructor's name.

To avoid future "Tip of the Tongue" experiences apply the Same-Sounds Meaning Cue to aid retrieval of the instructor's name, Jim. The following is an example of how to apply the Same-Sounds Meaning Cue Strategy to aid retrieval of someone's name.

Strategy Steps	Example
1. Identify the target name.	Target Name = Jim
2. Using the Same-Sounds Meaning Cue, associate the target name with a prompt word or phrase that both sounds like the target name and is linked in meaning to the target name.	*Same-Sounds Cue:* Link Jim to the word *gym* because the name Jim and the word *gym* sound the same when pronounced. *Meaning Cue: Gym* is also a meaning cue because you know that Jim works out at the *gym*.
3. Review this link between the Same-Sounds Meaning Cue and the target name by thinking of the prompt word immediately before saying the target name out loud.	Think of the cue *gym* immediately before saying the name Jim aloud. (…gym) **"Jim"**
4. Rehearse application of this strategy in three sentences or until you feel that you have overpracticed the target name and will retrieve it consistently.	Think of the cue immediately before saying the target name aloud in three sentences. 1. (…gym) **"Jim is very helpful."** 2. (…gym) **"Jim is very knowledgeable."** 3. (…gym) **"Jim is a great consultant."**

Practice Chart for Applying the Same-Sounds Meaning Cue Strategy

Select a proper name that has either caused you or may cause you to have a "Tip of the Tongue" word-finding error. For initial practice only, apply the Same-Sounds Meaning Cue Strategy to this name by completing the following chart.

Strategy Steps	Fill In the Blanks
1. Identify the target name.	Target Name = _____
2. Using the Same-Sounds Meaning Cue, associate the target name with a prompt word or phrase that both sounds like the target name and is linked in meaning to the target name.	*Same-Sounds Cue:* Link _____ (target name) to _____ (cue) because the name and the word each begin with the same first sounds. *Meaning Cue:* _____ is also a meaning cue because _____.
3. Review this link between the Same-Sounds Meaning Cue and the target name by thinking of the prompt word immediately before saying the target name out loud.	Think of _____ (cue) immediately before saying _____ (target name) aloud.
4. Write three sentences with the target name. Rehearse applying the Same-Sounds Meaning Cue Strategy in these sentences or until you feel that you have overpracticed the target name and will retrieve it consistently.	Think of _____ (cue) immediately before saying _____ (target name) aloud in the three sentences. 1. _____ 2. _____ 3. _____

Familiar-Word Cue Strategy

Um... uh...excuse me. I would like to participate.

Let's assume you were at a meeting Monday night. You started to address Barbie, the chairperson. You momentarily forgot her name and had a "Tip of the Tongue" experience.

The Familiar-Word Cue Strategy can also be used to improve your retrieval of personal names. To avoid having a "Tip of the Tongue" experience such as the preceding example, use the Familiar-Word Cue Strategy.

Figure 9.2 illustrates the application of the Familiar-Word Cue Strategy to aid retrieval of proper names.

Strategy Steps	Example
1. Identify the target name.	Target Name = Barbie
2. Using the Familiar-Word Cue, associate the target name with a prompt word that frequently co-occurs with the target name in other contexts.	Link Barbie to the words *Barbie doll* because the word *doll* is often said with the name Barbie.
3. Review this link between the Familiar-Word Cue and the target name by thinking of the prompt word(s) immediately before saying the target name out loud.	Think of the cue *Barbie doll* immediately before saying Barbie aloud. (…Barbie doll) **"Barbie"**
4. Rehearse application of this strategy in three sentences or until you feel that you have overpracticed the target name and will retrieve it consistently.	Think of the cue immediately before saying the target name aloud in three sentences. 1. (…Barbie doll) **"Barbie is very organized."** 2. (…Barbie doll) **"Barbie is a good leader."** 3. (…Barbie doll) **"Barbie is a smart woman."**

Figure 9.2. Using the Familiar-Word Cue Strategy to Reduce "Tip of the Tongue" Word-Finding Errors with Proper Names

Word-Finding Error	Word-Finding Strategy	Application of Strategy	Rehearse Word-Finding Strategy in Three Sentences
You have a "Tip of the Tongue" experience when you try to retrieve the name James. (Mind goes blank when you want to refer to your neighbor, James.)	**Familiar Word Cue** Link James to *James Bond* because Bond has been said with the name James in another context.	Think of the Familiar-Word Cue *James Bond* before saying the target name **"James"** aloud.	Think of the Familiar-Word Cue *James Bond* before saying the target name **"James"** aloud in several sentences. 1. **"I hope** (…James Bond) **James will be at the party."** 2. (…James Bond) **"James is my neighbor."** 3. **"Yesterday, I saw** (…James Bond) **James."**

Practice Chart for Applying the Familiar-Word Cue Strategy

Select a proper name that has either caused you or may cause you to have a "Tip of the Tongue" word-finding error. For initial practice only, apply the Familiar-Word Cue Strategy to this name by completing the following chart.

Strategy Steps	Fill In the Blanks
1. Identify the target name.	Target Name = _____
2. Using the Familiar-Word Cue, associate the target name with a prompt word that frequently co-occurs with the target name in other contexts.	Link _____ (target name) to _____ (cue) because _____ (cue) is often said with _____ (target name).
3. Review this link between the Familiar-Word Cue and the target name by thinking of the prompt word(s) immediately before saying the target name out loud.	Think of _____ (cue) immediately before saying _____ (target name) aloud.
4. Write three sentences with the target name. Rehearse applying the Familiar-Word Cue Strategy in these sentences or until you feel that you have overpracticed the target name and will retrieve it consistently.	Think of _____ (cue) immediately before saying _____ (target name) aloud in the three sentences. 1. _____ 2. _____ 3. _____

Examples of Applying Word-Finding Strategies to Reduce "Tip of the Tongue" Experiences with Names of Places, Events, and Entities

The meat was cooked on the... thing-a-ma-jig... oh....

Mary was explaining to her guests how the chicken entree was cooked. However, she had a "Tip of the Tongue" experience when she tried to retrieve the word *rotisserie*. She momentarily forgot the name of the appliance substituting the slang phrase "thing-a-ma-jig." The following cueing strategies can help Mary in future conversations when she has to retrieve object names.

This section presents strategies to reduce "Tip of the Tongue" experiences with names of places and entities that you know. These may be names of institutions, cities, medicines, movies, or books. Even though these are names of places, events, or things that you know and have said before, you may momentarily forget them just when you need to retrieve them. Similar to how you feel when you cannot remember personal names, you may feel that you have the name on the tip of your tongue.

I want to buy...those yellow flowers...oh....

Sharon was at the flower nursery when she had a "Tip of the Tongue" experience as she tried to tell the salesman that she wanted to buy daffodil bulbs.

Same-Sounds Cue Strategy

Sharon could benefit from using the Same-Sounds Cue Strategy to aid her retrieval of the flower name, daffodil. Use the following steps when applying the Same-Sounds Cue Strategy to improve retrieval of the names of entities, such as plants.

Strategy Steps	Example
1. Identify the target name.	Target Name = daffodil
2. Using the Same-Sounds Cue, link the target name with a prompt word or phrase that sounds like the target name.	*Same-Sounds Cue:* Link daffodil to the word *daffy* because the word *daffy* and the name daffodil each begin with the same first sounds.
3. Review this link between the Same-Sounds Cue and the target name by thinking of the prompt word immediately before saying the target name out loud.	Think of the cue *daffy* immediately before saying daffodil aloud. (…daffy) **"Daffodil"**
4. Rehearse application of this strategy in three sentences or until you feel that you have overpracticed the target name and will retrieve it consistently.	Think of the cue immediately before saying the target name aloud in three sentences. 1. **"The** (…daffy) **daffodils bloom in the spring."** 2. **"A** (…daffy) **daffodil bulb is planted in the fall."** 3. **"The** (…daffy) **daffodil is one of my favorite flowers."**

It is coming next year. It's …um…it's…our favorite.

Lee had a "Tip of the Tongue" experience when she was informing John that *Carmen* was coming to the opera house next year.

Lee could use the Same-Sounds Cue Strategy to aid her retrieval of the opera name, *Carmen*. Use the following steps when applying the Same-Sounds Cue Strategy to improve retrieval of names of events.

Strategy Steps	Example
1. Identify the target name.	Target Name = *Carmen*
2. Using the Same-Sounds Cue, link the target name with a prompt word or phrase that sounds like the target name.	*Same-Sounds Cue:* Link *Carmen* to the word *car* because *car* and *Carmen* have the same sounds in the first syllable.
3. Review this link between the Same-Sounds Cue and the target name by thinking of the prompt word immediately before saying the target name out loud.	Think of the cue *car* immediately before saying *Carmen* aloud. (...car) **"Carmen"**
4. Rehearse application of this strategy in three sentences or until you feel that you have overpracticed the target name and will retrieve it consistently.	Think of the cue *car* immediately before saying the target name aloud in three sentences. 1. (...car) **"Carmen is my favorite opera."** 2. **"I am going to see** (...car) **Carmen next year."** 3. (...car) **"Carmen is an exciting opera."**

Practice Chart for Applying the Same-Sounds Cue Strategy

Select the name of a place, event, or entity that has either caused you or may cause you to have a "Tip of the Tongue" word-finding error. For initial practice only, apply the Same-Sounds Cue Strategy to this name by completing the following chart.

Strategy Steps	Fill In the Blanks
1. Identify the target name.	Target Name = _____
2. Using the Same-Sounds Cue, link the target name with a prompt word or phrase that sounds like the target name.	*Same-Sounds Cue:* Link _____ (target name) to _____ (cue) because the target name and the cue word each begin with the same first sounds.
3. Review this link between the Same-Sounds Cue and the target name by thinking of the prompt word immediately before saying the target name out loud.	Think of _____ (cue) immediately before saying _____ (target name) aloud.
4. Write three sentences with the target name. Rehearse applying the Same-Sounds Cue Strategy in these sentences or until you feel that you have overpracticed the target name and will retrieve it consistently.	Think of _____ (cue) immediately before saying _____ (target name) aloud in the three sentences. 1. _____ 2. _____ 3. _____

Same-Sounds Meaning Cue Strategy

The Same-Sounds Meaning Cue Strategy is also recommended to improve your retrieval of names of movies, operas, or other titles that you know but may momentarily forget.

I just read The Waste Land by...um....

Let's assume you just read *The Waste Land* by T. S. Elliot. You want to be sure to retrieve both the title and the author's name when you talk about it.

To prevent having a "Tip of the Tongue" experience when you share what you are reading with others, use the Same-Sounds Meaning Cue Strategy. Use the following steps to anchor your retrieval of author's names.

Strategy Steps	Example
1. Identify the target name.	Target Name = T. S. Elliott
2. Using the Same-Sounds Meaning Cue, associate the target name with a prompt word or phrase that both sounds like the target name and is linked in meaning to the target name.	*Same-Sounds Cue:* Link the author's name Elliott to your friend's name Ellie because the names begin with the same first sounds. *Meaning Cue:* Ellie is also a meaning cue because you judge Ellie to be wasteful and the title of T. S. Elliott's work contains the word *waste*.
3. Review this link between the Same-Sounds Meaning Cue and the target name by thinking of the prompt word immediately before saying the target name out loud.	Think of the cue *Ellie* immediately before saying T. S. Elliott aloud. (…Ellie) **"T. S. Elliott"**
4. Rehearse application of this strategy in three sentences or until you feel that you have overpracticed the target name and will retrieve it consistently.	Think of the cue immediately before saying the target name aloud in three sentences. 1. (…Ellie) **"T. S. Elliott is the author of *The Waste Land.*"** 2. (…Ellie) **"T. S. Elliott is a great writer."** 3. (…Ellie) **"T. S. Elliott is my favorite poet."**

Practice Chart for Applying the Same-Sounds Meaning Cue Strategy

Select a name of a place, an event, or an entity that has either caused you or may cause you to have a "Tip of the Tongue" word-finding error. For initial practice only, apply the Same-Sounds Meaning Cue Strategy to this name by completing the following chart.

Strategy Steps	Fill In the Blanks
1. Identify the target name.	Target Name = _____
2. Using the Same-Sounds Meaning Cue, associate the target name with a prompt word or phrase that both sounds like the target name and is linked in meaning to the target name.	*Same-Sounds Cue:* Link _____ (target name) to _____ (cue) because the target name and the cue word each begin with the same first sounds. *Meaning Cue:* _____ is also a meaning cue because _____ .
3. Review this link between the Same-Sounds Meaning Cue and the target name by thinking of the prompt word immediately before saying the target name out loud.	Think of _____ (cue) immediately before saying _____ (target name) aloud.
4. Write three sentences with the target name. Rehearse applying the Same-Sounds Meaning Cue Strategy in these sentences or until you feel that you have overpracticed the target name and will retrieve it consistently.	Think of _____ (cue) immediately before saying _____ (target name) aloud in three sentences. 1. _____ 2. _____ 3. _____

Familiar-Word Cue Strategy

The Familiar-Word Cue can also be used to improve your retrieval of names of places, events, and entities that you know but may momentarily forget.

Let's assume that you just bought the stock of a company called Cisco. You want to be sure to be able to retrieve the name of the company when you tell your friends about this investment.

To prevent having a "Tip of the Tongue" experience when you share your investment with others, use the Familiar-Word Cue Strategy. Use the following steps to anchor your retrieval of the name of the stock you purchased.

Strategy Steps	Example
1. Identify the target name.	Target Name = Cisco
2. Using the Familiar-Word Cue, associate the target name with a prompt word that frequently co-occurs with the target name in other contexts.	Link Cisco to the words *Cisco Kid* because the word *kid* is often said with the name Cisco when referring to the cowboy legend, the Cisco Kid.
3. Review this link between the Familiar-Word Cue and the target name by thinking of the prompt word(s) immediately before saying the target name out loud.	Think of the cue *Cisco Kid* immediately before saying Cisco aloud. (...Cisco Kid) **"Cisco"**

Continued on next page

Strategy Steps	Example
4. Rehearse application of this strategy in three sentences or until you feel that you have overpracticed the target name and will retrieve it consistently.	Think of the cue immediately before saying the target name aloud in three sentences. 1. (…Cisco Kid) **"Cisco is a strong company."** 2. (…Cisco Kid) **"Cisco is a technology stock."** 3. **"I hope my** (…Cisco Kid) **Cisco stock splits."**

Same-Sounds Cue Strategy and the Familiar-Word Cue Strategy

The Same-Sounds Cue Strategy and the Familiar-Word Cue Strategy can be used together to improve your retrieval of names of places, events or entities that you know but may momentarily forget. The following example illustrates how to use these two strategies together to aid your retrieval of names of places.

We just got back from hiking at…uh…um….

Let's assume that you just returned from hiking at Sugar Loaf USA in Maine. You want to tell your friends, Lane and Sue, about your trip.

To prevent having a "Tip of the Tongue" experience when you tell your friends about your hiking adventure, use both the Same-Sounds Cue Strategy and the Familiar-Word Cue Strategy. Use the following steps to anchor your retrieval of the name of the place where you went hiking.

Strategy Steps	Example
1. Identify the target name.	Target Name = Sugar Loaf USA
2. Using the Same-Sounds Cue, link the target name with a prompt word or phrase that sounds like the target name. Using the Familiar-Word Cue, associate the target name with a prompt word that frequently co-occurs with the target name in other contexts.	*Same-Sounds Cue:* Link Sugar to the sweetener *sugar* because the word *sugar* is repeated. *Familiar-Word Cue:* Link Loaf to the phrase *loaf of bread* because the word *loaf* is said with the word *bread* in the phrase loaf of bread.
3. Review these links between the cues and the target name by thinking of the prompt words immediately before saying the target name out loud.	Think of the cue words *sugar* and *loaf of bread* immediately before saying Sugar Loaf USA aloud. (...sugar, loaf of bread) **"Sugar Loaf USA"**
4. Rehearse application of these strategies in three sentences or until you feel that you have overpracticed the target name and will retrieve it consistently.	Think of the cues immediately before saying the target name aloud in three sentences. 1. (...sugar, loaf of bread) **"Sugar Loaf USA is a beautiful spot."** 2. (...sugar, loaf of bread) **"Sugar Loaf USA is in Maine."** 3. (...sugar, loaf of bread) **"Sugar Loaf USA is a great place to hike."**

Practice Chart for Applying the Familiar-Word Cue Strategy

Select the name of a place, event, or entity that has either caused you or may cause you to have a "Tip of the Tongue" word-finding error. For initial practice only, apply the Familiar-Word Cue Strategy to this name by completing the following chart.

Strategy Steps	Fill In the Blanks
1. Identify the target name.	Target Name = _____
2. Using the Familiar-Word Cue, associate the target name with a prompt word that frequently co-occurs with the target name in other contexts.	Link _____ (target name) to _____ (cue) because _____ (cue) is often said with _____ (target name).
3. Review this link between the Familiar-Word Cue and the target name by thinking of the prompt word(s) immediately before saying the target name out loud.	Think of _____ (cue) immediately before saying _____ (target name) aloud.
4. Write three sentences with the target name. Rehearse applying the Familiar-Word Cue Strategy in these sentences or until you feel that you have overpracticed the target name and will retrieve it consistently.	Think of _____ (cue) immediately before saying _____ (target name) aloud in the three sentences. 1. _____ 2. _____ 3. _____

Examples of Applying Word-Finding Strategies to Reduce "Tip of the Tongue" Experiences with Common Words

I like to sing a...oh...you know ...to my nieces at bedtime.

Donna had a "Tip of the Tongue" experience when telling her friends how she puts her nieces to sleep. She could not think of the word *lullaby*. The following word-finding strategies can help her anchor retrieval of the target word.

This section presents examples of how to apply word-finding strategies to reduce "Tip of the Tongue" experiences when you are retrieving common nouns, verbs, adjectives, or adverbs. When an individual has a "Tip of the Tongue" experience with a common word, it is often not thought to be a difficulty in word finding. Instead, it is perceived as a lack of knowledge (i.e., not knowing the target word). Yet failures to retrieve common words can really be word-finding disruptions when they occur with words the person knows and has used correctly in other contexts.

We bought our niece a beautiful...uh ...thingy.

Let's assume you were telling your friends what you bought your niece for graduation. In your description you were unable to retrieve the noun *pendant*. Use the following steps to apply the Same-Sounds Cue Strategy to improve future retrieval of this word.

Same-Sounds Cue Strategy

The Same-Sounds Cue Strategy can aid your retrieval of common words. The following example illustrates how to apply the Same-Sounds Cue to aid future retrieval of the word *pendant*.

Strategy Steps	Example
1. Identify the target noun.	Target Noun = pendant
2. Using the Same-Sounds Cue, link the target noun with a prompt word or phrase that sounds like the target noun.	*Same-Sounds Cue:* Link pendant to the word *pending* because the word *pending* and the word *pendant* each begin with the same first sounds.
3. Review this link between the Same-Sounds Cue and the target noun by thinking of the prompt word immediately before saying the target noun out loud.	Think of the cue *pending* immediately before saying the target noun *pendant* aloud. (...pending) **"Pendant"**
4. Rehearse application of this strategy in three sentences or until you feel that you have overpracticed the target noun and will retrieve it consistently.	Think of the cue immediately before saying the target noun aloud in three sentences. 1. **"The** (...pending) **pendant is a blue topaz."** 2. **"The** (...pending) **pendant is on a gold chain."** 3. **"The** (...pending) **pendant is something she can where on special occasions."**

Practice Chart for Applying the Same-Sounds Cue Strategy

Select a common noun that has either caused you or may cause you to have a "Tip of the Tongue" word-finding error. For initial practice only, apply the Same-Sounds Cue Strategy to this word by completing the following chart.

Strategy Steps	Fill In the Blanks
1. Identify the target word.	Target Word = _____
2. Using the Same-Sounds Cue, link the target word with a prompt word or phrase that sounds like the target word.	*Same-Sounds Cue:* Link _____ (target word) to _____ (cue) because the target word and the cue word each begin with the same first sounds.
3. Review this link between the Same-Sounds Cue and the target word by thinking of the prompt word immediately before saying the target word out loud.	Think of _____ (cue) immediately before saying _____ (target word) aloud.
4. Write three sentences with the target word. Rehearse applying the Same-Sounds Cue Strategy in these sentences or until you feel that you have overpracticed the target word and will retrieve it consistently.	Think of _____ (cue) immediately before saying _____ (target word) aloud in the three sentences. 1. _____ 2. _____ 3. _____

I am going to wear my black ...you know...my new pants.

Sherry had a "Tip of the Tongue" experience when she tried to tell her partner Michael what she was going to wear. She could not retrieve the word *corduroy.*

Same-Sounds Meaning Cue Strategy

The Same-Sounds Meaning Cue Strategy can also aid your retrieval of common words. The following example illustrates how Sherry could apply the Same-Sounds Meaning Cue to aid her future retrieval of the target word *corduroy*.

Strategy Steps	Example
1. Identify the target noun.	Target Noun = corduroy
2. Using the Same-Sounds Meaning Cue, associate the target noun with a prompt word or phrase that both sounds like the target noun and is linked in meaning to the target noun.	*Same-Sounds Cue:* Link corduroy to the word *cord* because the words *corduroy* and *cord* each begin with the same initial sounds. *Meaning Cue:* The word *cord* is also a meaning cue because corduroy is a cloth with rib-like cords on its surface.
3. Review this link between the Same-Sounds Meaning Cue and the target noun by thinking of the prompt word immediately before saying the target noun out loud.	Think of the cue *cord* immediately before saying the target noun *corduroy* aloud. (…cord) **"Corduroy"**
4. Rehearse application of this strategy in three sentences or until you feel that you have overpracticed the target noun and will retrieve it consistently.	Think of the cue immediately before saying the target noun aloud in three sentences. 1. **"I am going to wear my new** (…cord) **corduroys."** 2. (…cord) **"Corduroy is warm."** 3. (…cord) **"Corduroy is a sturdy fabric."**

Practice Chart for Applying the Same-Sounds Meaning Cue Strategy

Select a common noun that has either caused you or may cause you to have a "Tip of the Tongue" word-finding error. For initial practice only, apply the Same-Sounds Meaning Cue Strategy to this word by completing the following chart.

Strategy Steps	Fill In the Blanks
1. Identify the target word.	Target Word = _____
2. Using the Same-Sounds Meaning Cue, associate the target word with a prompt word or phrase that both sounds like the target word and is linked in meaning to the target word.	*Same-Sounds Cue:* Link _____ (target word) to _____ (cue) because the target word and the cue word each begin with the same first sounds. *Meaning Cue:* _____ is also a meaning cue because _____ .
3. Review this link between the Same-Sounds Meaning Cue and the target word by thinking of the prompt word immediately before saying the target word out loud.	Think of _____ (cue) immediately before saying _____ (target word) aloud.
4. Write three sentences with the target word. Rehearse applying the Same-Sounds Meaning Cue Strategy in these sentences or until you feel that you have overpracticed the target name and will retrieve it consistently.	Think of _____ (cue) immediately before saying _____ (target word) aloud in three sentences. 1. _____ 2. _____ 3. _____

Have you seen my...um...um...the thing for my glasses?

Let's assume that you were looking for the cord that you put around your neck to hold your glasses. You have a "Tip of the Tongue" experience when you ask your daughter if she has seen it.

Familiar-Word Cue Strategy

The Familiar-Word Cue Strategy can also help reduce "Tip of the Tongue" word-finding errors with common words. Use the following steps to link a Familiar-Word Cue to the target word, *cord,* to aid your retrieval of that target noun.

Strategy Steps	Example
1. Identify the target noun.	Target Noun = cord
2. Using the Familiar-Word Cue, associate the target noun with a prompt word that frequently co-occurs with the target noun in other contexts.	Link cord to the word *spinal* because the word *spinal* is often said with the word *cord* in a different context (i.e., spinal cord).
3. Review this link between the Familiar-Word Cue and the target noun by thinking of the prompt word(s) immediately before saying the target noun out loud.	Think of the cue *spinal* immediately before saying the target noun *cord* aloud. (...spinal) **"Cord"**
4. Rehearse application of this strategy in three sentences or until you feel that you have overpracticed the target noun and will retrieve it consistently.	Think of the cue immediately before saying the target noun aloud in three sentences. 1. **"I can't find the** (...spinal) **cord for my glasses."** 2. **"I need to buy a yellow** (...spinal) **cord for my glasses."** 3. **"I think I will put the beaded** (...spinal) **cord on my glasses."**

Practice Chart for Applying the Familiar-Word Cue Strategy

Select a common word that has either caused you or may cause you to have a "Tip of the Tongue" word-finding error. For initial practice only, apply the Familiar-Word Cue Strategy to this word by completing the following chart.

Strategy Steps	Fill In the Blanks
1. Identify the target word.	Target Word = _____
2. Using the Familiar-Word Cue, associate the target word with a prompt word that frequently co-occurs with the target word in other contexts.	Link _____ (target word) to _____ (cue) because _____ (cue) is often said with _____ (target word).
3. Review this link between the Familiar-Word Cue and the target word by thinking of the prompt word(s) immediately before saying the target word out loud.	Think of _____ (cue) immediately before saying _____ (target word) aloud.
4. Write three sentences with the target word. Rehearse applying the Familiar-Word Cue Strategy in these sentences or until you feel that you have overpracticed the target word and will retrieve it consistently.	Think of _____ (cue) immediately before saying _____ (target word) aloud in the three sentences. 1. _____ 2. _____ 3. _____

Synonym or Category-Name Substituting Strategy

The Synonym or Category-Name Substituting Strategy can improve your communication when you think that you are going to have a word-finding difficulty. The following are steps to use to circumvent a "Tip of the Tongue" experience.

I feel...um ...like I have no power in this situation.

Let's assume that you are explaining to a coworker how you feel about a situation at work. As you are talking, you are unable to retrieve the word *ineffectual*.

Instead of describing how you feel in this example, you could switch to a synonym for the target word. You could substitute the word *powerless* for the elusive adverb. Use the following steps to apply the Synonym-Substituting Strategy for the target word.

Strategy Steps	Example
1. While you are talking, think ahead to identify the elusive word that you may have trouble retrieving.	Elusive Word = ineffectual
2. Think of a word that is similar in meaning to the elusive word.	powerless
3. Using the Synonym-Substituting Strategy, substitute the synonym for the elusive target word.	Substitute the word *powerless* for the target word *ineffectual*.

Continued on next page

Strategy Steps	Example
4. Complete the sentence inserting the synonym in place of the target word while you are talking.	**"I feel powerless in this situation."**
5. Rehearse application of this strategy prior to an event by thinking of synonyms or alternate words for target words or names that you think you might have difficulty retrieving.	

Final Guidelines for Applying Strategies to Reduce "Tip of the Tongue" Experiences

This chapter presents final guidelines for applying word-finding strategies to improve retrieval of names and words you know. Following these guidelines, try each strategy in Chapter 9 to determine which ones are most appropriate for your word-finding style. Once you determine which strategies help you say a name or word automatically, use those strategies consistently to aid your retrieval of names and words.

Final Guidelines

- Identify the specific names or words that you had difficulty retrieving.
- If these are names or words you know and have said before, establish and apply the word-finding strategies as soon as you identify the elusive target words.
- If these are names or words you have recently learned, establish and apply the word-finding strategies soon after you have learned these words. For example,

  a) If it is the name of a city, then apply retrieval cues just after you have learned the name of that city.

  b) If it is the name of a medicine, apply the retrieval cues just after you have learned the medicine name.

  c) If it a name of a book or movie, apply retrieval cues just after you have learned the book or movie name.

  d) If it is general vocabulary, apply retrieval cues just after you have learned the words.

- Whenever applying the word-finding strategies, always rehearse by first thinking of the cue (do not say the cue aloud) and then saying the target word aloud, first in isolation and then in a sentence.
- If you applied an Association Cue Strategy, review the strategy by thinking of the cue and saying aloud the target word alone and in a sentence.

- If applying the Association Cue Strategy because you had a "Tip of the Tongue" experience, make the associations to the elusive word as soon as you recall it.

- If using the Association Cue Strategies to prevent having a "Tip of the Tongue" experience at an upcoming event, apply the strategy the night before or on the way to the event.

- If you applied the Synonym or Category-Name Substituting Strategy, rehearse aloud sentences with the target word and with the alternate word.

Once you have followed these guidelines and applied a strategy to a particular name or word, you will typically have success in retrieving (saying) that name or word accurately in other speaking situations. However, if you find that you are still having difficulty with that name or word, reapply and rehearse the chosen strategy.

PART 5

The "Twist of the Tongue" Word-Finding Error

Getting Started

The...forsisia ...um...forsythia are blooming.

You were explaining to your granddaughter that each spring the forsythia bloom in the front yard. In teaching her about this spring flower, you made a "Twist of the Tongue" error because you momentarily forgot the sounds of that flower name.

Incorrectly saying names and words that are three or more syllables in length is another type of word-finding difficulty. Even though these are names and words you know and have said before, you say them incorrectly recalling only some of their sounds. Some people report, "These long names or words just don't roll off my tongue the way they used to." Such difficulty with long names and words are often examples of the "Twist of the Tongue" word-finding error.

This chapter indicates behaviors that will help you successfully handle a "Twist of the Tongue" experience when you are talking as well as aid you in reducing future difficulties with word finding. Using the following list will help you present your ideas without stops and hesitations and allow you to be at your personal best when you are speaking.

1. While talking, if you identify a long word with sounds that you will have difficulty retrieving, substitute a synonym or category for the target word to keep from making a "Twist of the Tongue" error.

2. Refrain from ignoring word-finding difficulties that you have with names or words that are three or more syllables in length.

3. Apply the strategies in Chapter 12 to these long names or words that were difficult for you to retrieve in earlier conversations.

4. Plan ahead! Identify names and words that are three or four syllables in length that you may have difficulty retrieving in upcoming conversations.

5. Apply the strategies in Chapter 12 to help you retrieve these longer names and words in future conversations.

6. Refrain from saying, "I can't say those long words" or mumbling long words whose sounds you are not able to retrieve. These behaviors call attention to your word-finding difficulty.

Strategies to Reduce "Twists of the Tongue" with Names and Common Words

Her name is…Bec…Beclihe …something like that.

Ethel was telling her neighbor about the new resident who just moved into the retirement community. Ethel had a "Twist of the Tongue" word-finding error as she tried to say the three syllable name Bechtolshem. Either of the following Syllable-Dividing Strategies can help Ethel and you become automatic in the retrieval of names three or more syllables in length.

This chapter presents examples of how to apply word-finding strategies to improve your ability to retrieve multisyllabic (three or more syllables in length) names and words. First, strategies recommended to reduce "Twists of the Tongue" word-finding errors with names and words are reviewed. These include Syllable Dividing, Same-Sounds Cue,

Alternate Word Cue, and Rehearsal Strategies. Second, examples of how to apply each of these strategies are presented. Third, practice charts are provided to help you automatically apply these strategies to names and words that have caused "Twist of the Tongue" word-finding errors. Figure 12.1 displays the word finding strategies recommended to reduce the "Twist of the Tongue" word finding error.

Visual or Rhythm Syllable-Dividing Strategy

When using Syllable-Dividing Strategies, you either draw a line between each syllable (Visual Syllable-Dividing) or mark each syllable with a rhythmic tap (Rhythm Syllable-Dividing) before rehearsing the word. Select either strategy to aid your retrieval of words three or more syllables in length.

Same-Sounds Cue Strategy

In this context, the Same-Sounds Cue Strategy directs the speaker to link each syllable of the target word, to a word that sounds like (shares similar sounds) the syllable.

Rehearsal Strategy

The Rehearsal Strategy involves rehearsing the target word by saying it aloud in isolation and in three sentences. *Note:* When using the Rehearsal Strategy with the Association Cue Strategies, *do not say* the chosen cue out loud. Think of the cue and then say

Figure 12.1. Word-Finding Strategies to Reduce "Twists of the Tongue"

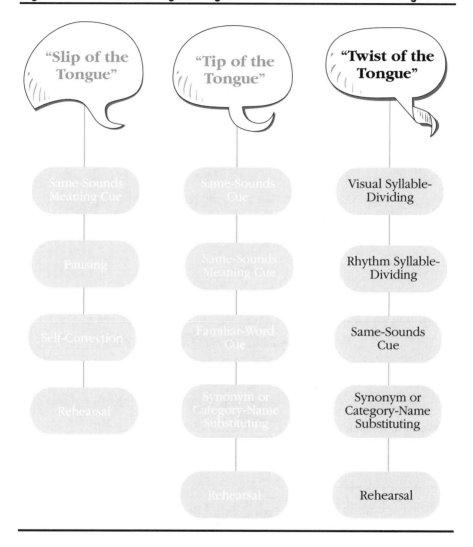

the target name or word aloud. Remember to always rehearse **out loud**. Rehearsing silently will not improve your word-finding skills when you are talking. Because the Rehearsal Strategy is used with all the word-finding strategies presented, application of this strategy is indicated with each of the word-finding strategies.

Synonym or Category-Name Substituting Strategy

The Synonym or Category-Name Substitution Strategy directs you to substitute a synonym or category name for the target word that you are unable to retrieve.

Examples of Applying Word-Finding Strategies to Reduce "Twist of the Tongue" Errors with Proper Names

I would like you to meet Ms. Zaw... Zeski....

Let's assume that your new neighbor's name is Ms. Zawojewski. You want to be able to retrieve her name correctly when you introduce her at your party this weekend.

Individuals report that they frequently have difficulty remembering all the sounds of long names when they are speaking. Since we frequently meet people whose names are three or more syllable in length, it is important that we are able to readily retrieve these names.

Syllable-Dividing Strategies are helpful in improving retrieval of multisyllabic names. In this example your neighbor's name, Zawojewski, is a four-syllable name. You would use one of the Syllable-Dividing Strategies to ensure correct and automatic retrieval of this name. The following steps are examples of how to apply the Visual and Rhythm Syllable-Dividing Strategies to aid retrieval of personal names that are three or more syllables in length.

Visual Syllable-Dividing

Strategy Steps	Example
1. Identify the target name.	Target Name = Zawojewski
2. Draw a line between each syllable.	Za / wo / jew / ski

Rhythm Syllable-Dividing

Strategy Steps	Example
1. Identify the target name.	Target Name = Zawojewski
2. As you say each syllable, mark it with a rhythmic tap to emphasize the syllables of the target name.	Make four rhythmic taps while you say: **"Za wo jew ski."** ∧ ∧ ∧ ∧
3. Rehearse the target name by saying each syllable out loud.	Say: **"Za / wo / jew / ski."**
4. Rehearse the target name as a unit three times or until you can say it automatically without hesitation.	Say the name Zawojewski three times. 1. **"Zawojewski"** 2. **"Zawojewski"** 3. **"Zawojewski"**
5. Rehearse saying the target name aloud in three sentences or until you feel that you will retrieve it consistently.	Rehearse the following three sentences. 1. **"My neighbor's last name is Zawojewski."** 2. **"Mrs. Zawojewski is my neighbor."** 3. **"I like the Zawojewski's home."**

Practice Charts for Applying the Syllable-Dividing Strategies

Select a proper name that has either caused you or may cause you to have a "Twist of the Tongue" word-finding error. For initial practice only, apply one of the Syllable-Dividing Strategies to this name by completing the following charts.

Visual Syllable-Dividing

Strategy Steps	Fill In the Blanks
1. Identify a target name that is three or more syllables in length.	Target Name = _____
2. Draw a line between each syllable.	____ / ____ / ____ / ____ / ____

Rhythm Syllable-Dividing

Strategy Steps	Fill In the Blanks
1. Identify a target name that is three or more syllables in length.	Target Name = _____
2. As you say each syllable, mark it with a rhythmic tap to emphasize the syllables of the target name.	Make rhythmic taps while you say: ____ ____ ____ ____ ∧ ∧ ∧ ∧
3. Rehearse the target name by saying each syllable out loud.	Say: ____ ____ ____ ____
4. Rehearse the target name as a unit three times or until you can say it automatically without hesitation.	1. _____ 2. _____ 3. _____

Continued on next page

Strategy Steps	Fill In the Blanks
5. Write three sentences with the target name. Rehearse these sentences until you feel that you have overpracticed the target name and will retrieve it consistently.	Rehearse the following three sentences. 1. _____ 2. _____ 3. _____

Same-Sounds Cue Strategy

The Same-Sounds Cue Strategy can be used along with the Syllable-Dividing Strategies to aid retrieval of target names three or more syllables in length.

I would like you to meet Mr. Ma...Macsy

Let's assume that a friend named Mr. Macaskill will be attending your party mentioned in the previous example. You also want to retrieve his name correctly when you introduce him to your other guests.

Link each syllable in Macaskill with a word that sounds like that syllable to anchor your retrieval of this name. Use the following steps to apply the Same-Sounds Cue to aid accurate retrieval of the personal name Macaskill and other names three or more syllables in length.

Strategy Steps	Example
1. Identify the target name.	Target Name = Macaskill
2. Using the Same-Sounds Cue, link each syllable of the target name with a prompt word that sounds like the syllable.	*Same-Sounds Cue:* Link the syllable / Mac / to the name *Mack* because the name Mack and the syllable / Mac / consist of the same sounds. Link the syllable / cask / to the word *cast* because the word *cast* and the syllable / cask / consist of some of the same sounds. Link the syllable / skill / to the word *skill* because the word *skill* and the syllable / skill / have the same sounds.
3. Review these links between the Same-Sounds Cues and the target name syllables by thinking of the prompt words immediately before saying the target name out loud.	Think of the cues *Mack-cast-skill* immediately before saying the target name Macaskill aloud. (…Mack-cast-skill) **"Macaskill"**
4. Rehearse application of this strategy in three sentences or until you feel that you have overpracticed the target name and will retrieve it consistently.	Think of the cues immediately before saying the target name aloud in three sentences. 1. (…Mack-cast-skill) **"Macaskill is the last name of my neighbor."** 2. (…Mack-cast-skill) **"Macaskill is a good friend."** 3. **"The** (…Mack-cast-skill) **Macaskill family is coming over."**

Figure 12.2 displays the use of Syllable-Dividing Strategies to aid retrieval of personal names that are three or more syllables in length.

Practice Chart for Applying the Same-Sounds Cue Strategy

Select a proper name that has either caused you or could cause you to have a "Twist of the Tongue"

Figure 12.2. Using Word-Finding Strategies to Reduce "Twists of the Tongue" When Retrieving Personal Names Three or More Syllables In Length

Word-Finding Error	Word-Finding Strategies	Application of Strategy	Rehearse Word-Finding Strategy in Three Sentences
Calling Mr. Marinski either Mr. Minski or Mr. Miski (omitting sounds).	**Visual Syllable-Dividing** Ma / rin / ski	1. After using the Visual or Rhythm Syllable-Dividing Strategy, practice saying Marinski syllable by syllable. **"Ma / rin / ski"** or **"Ma rin ski"** ᴧ ᴧ ᴧ 2. Practice saying Marinski as a unit three times. **"Marinski"** **"Marinski"** **"Marinski"**	Think of the cues *Ma-rinse-ski* before saying the target name out loud in a sentence. 1. **"I met Mr.** (…Ma-rinse-ski) **Marinski at the computer store yesterday."** 2. **"Mr.** (…Ma-rinse-ski) **Marinski is very knowledgeable about computers."** 3. **"I hope Mr.** (…Ma-rinse-ski) **Marinski joins us on the committee."**
	Rhythm Syllable-Dividing Ma rin ski ᴧ ᴧ ᴧ		
	Same-Sounds Cue Link / Ma / with *Ma*, link / rin / with *rinse*, and link / ski / with *ski*.	Think of the cue *Ma-rinse-ski* before saying the target name Marinski, aloud.	

word-finding error. For initial practice only, apply the
Same-Sounds Cue Strategy to this name by completing
the following chart.

Strategy Steps	Fill In the Blanks
1. Identify the target name.	Target Name = _____
2. Using the Same-Sounds Cue, link each syllable of the target name with a prompt word or phrase that sounds like the syllable.	*Same Sounds Cue:* Link _____ (target syllable) to _____ (cue) because the target syllable and the cue word each begin with the same first sounds. Link _____ (target syllable) to _____ (cue) because the target syllable and the cue word each begin with the same first sounds. Link _____ (target syllable) to _____ (cue) because the target syllable and the cue word each begin with the same first sounds. Link _____ (target syllable) to _____ (cue) because the target syllable and the cue word each begin with the same first sounds.
3. Review these links between the Same-Sounds Cues and the target name syllables by thinking of the prompt words immediately before saying the target name out loud.	Think of _____ (cues) immediately before saying _____ (target name) aloud.

Continued on next page

Strategy Steps	Fill In the Blanks
4. Write three sentences with the target name. Rehearse applying the Same-Sounds Cue Strategy in these sentences or until you feel that you have overpracticed the target name and will retrieve it consistently.	Think of _____ (cues) immediately before saying _____ (target name) aloud in three sentences. 1. _____ 2. _____ 3. _____

Examples of Applying Word-Finding Strategies to Reduce "Twist of the Tongue" Errors with Names of Places, Events, and Entities

Presented in this section are strategies to reduce the "Twist of the Tongue" word-finding error with names of known places, events, and things. Even though these may be names of institutions, cities, medicines, movies, or books that you know and have said before, you may mispronounce these words recalling only some of the sounds that make up these names. You might describe these long words as tongue twisters. Because these are names that you have said correctly in other contexts, these speaking errors may stem from a problem in retrieving all of the sounds of the target word and could be a word-finding error. The following are word-finding strategies to improve your ability to say the names of places, events, and things that are three or more syllables in length.

Can you fill a prescription for Mic...Micinclin?

Eva was requesting a refill for a prescription at the pharmacy. She had a "Twist of the Tongue" word-finding error as she tried to say the three syllable name of the medicine, Miacalcin. The following Syllable-Dividing Strategies can help Eva become automatic in her retrieval of medication names.

In this example, Eva had difficulty retrieving the medication name, Miacalcin, when she attempted to refill her prescription. Miacalcin, like many medication names, is four syllables in length and can be difficult to retrieve without making a "Twist of the Tongue" error. To ensure that you have automatic retrieval when you ask your pharmacist to fill your prescription, apply one of the Syllable-Dividing Strategies to medicine names before trying to say them. Using either the Visual or Rhythm Syllable-Dividing Strategy, complete the following steps to aid your retrieval of names that are three or more syllables in length.

Visual Syllable-Dividing

Strategy Steps	Example
1. Identify the target name.	Target Name = Miacalcin
2. Draw a line between each syllable.	Mi / a / cal / cin

Rhythm Syllable-Dividing

Strategy Steps	Example
1. Identify the target name.	Target Name = Miacalcin
2. As you say each syllable, mark it with a rhythmic tap to emphasize the syllables of the target name.	Make four rhythmic taps while you say: **"Mi a cal cin."** ∧ ∧ ∧ ∧
3. Rehearse the target name by saying each syllable out loud.	Say: **"Mi / a / cal / cin."**
4. Rehearse the target name as a unit three times or until you can say it automatically without hesitation.	Say Miacalcin three times. 1. **"Miacalcin"** 2. **"Miacalcin"** 3. **"Miacalcin"**
5. Rehearse saying the target name aloud in three sentences or until you feel that you will retrieve it consistently.	Rehearse the following three sentences. 1. **"I need to take Miacalcin."** 2. **"Miacalcin builds bone density."** 3. **"Miacalcin stops bone loss."**

We just returned from Apolis, I mean Annapolis.

Let's assume that you just returned from visiting family in Annapolis, Maryland and you want to tell your neighbors where you went. Because Annapolis is a four syllable word, you are worried that you might make a "Twist of the Tongue" word-finding error as you tell them about your trip.

To aid retrieval of the target name Annapolis, use the Visual or Rhythm Syllable-Dividing Strategies presented in the following steps.

Visual Syllable-Dividing

Strategy Steps	Example
1. Identify the target name.	Target Name = Annapolis
2. Draw a line between each syllable.	An / nap / o / lis

Rhythm Syllable-Dividing

Strategy Steps	Example
1. Identify the target name.	Target Name = Annapolis
2. As you say each syllable, mark it with a rhythmic tap to emphasize the syllables of the target name.	Make four rhythmic taps while you say: **"An nap o lis."** ^ ^ ^ ^
3. Rehearse the target name by saying each syllable out loud.	Say: **"An / nap / o / lis."**
4. Rehearse the target name as a unit three times or until you can say it automatically without hesitation.	Say Annapolis three times. 1. **"Annapolis"** 2. **"Annapolis"** 3. **"Annapolis"**
5. Rehearse saying the target name aloud in three sentences or until you feel that you will retrieve it consistently.	Rehearse the following three sentences. 1. **"We visited my family in Annapolis."** 2. **"Annapolis is an exciting city."** 3. **"Annapolis is the capital of Maryland."**

Practice Charts for Applying the Syllable-Dividing Strategies

Select the name of a place, event, or entity that has either caused you or may cause you to have a "Twist of the Tongue" word-finding error. For initial practice only, apply the Syllable-Dividing Strategies to this name by completing the following charts.

Visual Syllable-Dividing

Strategy Steps	Fill In the Blanks
1. Identify a target name that is three or more syllables in length.	Target Name = _____
2. Draw a line between each syllable.	_____ / _____ / _____ / _____ / _____

Rhythm Syllable-Dividing

Strategy Steps	Fill In the Blanks
1. Identify a target name that is three or more syllables in length.	Target Name = _____
2. As you say each syllable, mark it with a rhythmic tap to emphasize the syllables of the target name.	Make rhythmic taps while you say: ____ ____ ____ ____ ∧ ∧ ∧ ∧
3. Rehearse the target name by saying each syllable out loud.	Say: ____ ____ ____ ____
4. Rehearse the target name as a unit three times or until you can say it automatically without hesitation.	1. _____ 2. _____ 3. _____
5. Write three sentences with the target name. Rehearse these sentences until you feel that you have overpracticed the target name and will retrieve it consistently.	Rehearse the following three sentences. 1. _____ 2. _____ 3. _____

Same-Sounds Cue Strategy

After you have rehearsed the production of a long name you may also want to use the Same-Sounds Cue to aid your retrieval of this name. The following is an example of how to apply this strategy to a city name four syllables in length.

Strategy Steps	Example
1. Identify the target name.	Target Name = Annapolis
2. Using the Same-Sounds Cue, link each syllable of the target name with a prompt word that sounds like the syllable.	*Same-Sounds Cue:* Link the syllable / An / to the name *Ann* because the name Ann and the syllable / An / have the same sounds. Link the syllables / nap / o / lis / to the word *apple* because the word *apple* and the syllables / nap / o / lis / have similar sounds.
3. Review these links between the Same-Sounds Cues and the target name syllables by thinking of the prompt words immediately before saying the target name out loud.	Think of the cues *Ann* and *apples* immediately before saying the target name Annapolis aloud. (...Ann, apples) **"Annapolis"**
4. Rehearse application of this strategy in three sentences or until you feel that you have overpracticed the target name and will retrieve it consistently.	Think of the cues immediately before saying the target name aloud in three sentences. 1. **"We visited my family in** (Ann, apples) **Annapolis."** 2. (Ann, apples) **"Annapolis is an exciting city."** 3. (Ann, apples) **"Annapolis is the capital of Maryland."**

Practice Chart for Applying the Same-Sounds Cue Strategy

Select the name of a place, event, or entity that has either caused you or may cause you to have a "Twist of the Tongue" word-finding error. For initial practice only, apply the Same-Sounds Cue Strategy to this name by completing the following chart.

Strategy Steps	Fill In the Blanks
1. Identify the target name.	Target Name = _____
2. Using the Same-Sounds Cue, link each syllable of the target name with a prompt word or phrase that sounds like the syllable.	*Same Sounds Cue:* Link _____ (target syllable) to _____ (cue) because the target syllable and the cue word each begin with the same first sounds. Link _____ (target syllable) to _____ (cue) because the target syllable and the cue word each begin with the same first sounds. Link _____ (target syllable) to _____ (cue) because the target syllable and the cue word each begin with the same first sounds. Link _____ (target syllable) to _____ (cue) because the target syllable and the cue word each begin with the same first sounds.

Continued on next page

Strategy Steps	Fill In the Blanks
3. Review these links between the Same-Sounds Cues and the target name syllables by thinking of the prompt words immediately before saying the target name out loud.	Think of _____ (cues) immediately before saying _____ (target name) aloud.
4. Write three sentences with the target name. Rehearse applying the Same-Sounds Cue Strategy in these sentences or until you feel that you have overpracticed the target name and will retrieve it consistently.	Think of _____ (cues) immediately before saying _____ (target name) aloud in three sentences. 1. _____ 2. _____ 3. _____

Examples of Applying Word-Finding Strategies to Reduce "Twist of the Tongue" Errors with Common Words

Make the candles using... pafin...paraffin.

Toby was explaining to her students what they will be using to make the candles for the class project. She made a "Twist of the Tongue" word-finding error as she tried to say the three syllable word *paraffin*. Either of the following Syllable-Dividing Strategies can help Toby become automatic in her retrieval of words three or more syllables in length.

In a conversation you may have difficulty retrieving common nouns, verbs, adjectives, and adverbs that are three or more syllables in length. These twists of the tongue are typically overlooked by listeners as temporary confusion. Even so, these speaking errors often stem from a problem in retrieving all of the sounds of the target word. Because these errors occur with words that a person knows and has used correctly in other contexts, these may be word-finding disruptions. It is necessary to practice saying these longer words to reduce "Twist of the Tongue" word-finding errors. This section presents examples of how to apply word-finding strategies to improve your ability to retrieve common words that are three or more syllables in length.

Let's assume you had difficulty retrieving the four syllable word *animation* when you were describing the process used to create cartoons. To improve your word-finding skills with this word or other long words use the following steps.

Visual Syllable-Dividing

Strategy Steps	Example
1. Identify the target word.	Target Word = animation
2. Draw a line between each syllable.	an / i / ma / tion

Rhythm Syllable-Dividing

Strategy Steps	Example
1. Identify the target word.	Target Word = animation
2. As you say each syllable, mark it with a rhythmic tap to emphasize the syllables of the target word.	Make four rhythmic taps while you say: **"An i ma tion."** ^ ^ ^ ^
3. Rehearse the target word by saying each syllable out loud.	Say: **"An / i / ma / tion."**
4. Rehearse the target word as a unit three times or until you can say it automatically without hesitation.	Say animation three times. 1. **"Animation"** 2. **"Animation"** 3. **"Animation"**
5. Rehearse saying the target word aloud in three sentences or until you feel that you will retrieve it consistently.	Rehearse the following three sentences. 1. **"Today, animation is done on computers."** 2. **"Animation is an art form."** 3. **"I need animation software."**

Your skills are immemory...

Let's assume you are at an award ceremony. In your introduction of the speaker, you had difficulty retrieving the adjective *immeasurable*. To improve your word-finding skills with this word, use one of the Syllable-Dividing Strategies. Use the following steps to aid your retrieval of this and other words that are three or more syllables in length.

Visual Syllable-Dividing

Strategy Steps	Example
1. Identify the target word.	Target Word = immeasurable
2. Draw a line between each syllable.	im / meas / ur / a / ble

Rhythm Syllable-Dividing

Strategy Steps	Example
1. Identify the target word.	Target Word = immeasurable
2. As you say each syllable, mark it with a rhythmic tap to emphasize the syllables of the target word.	Make five rhythmic taps while you say: **"Im meas ur a ble."** ∧ ∧ ∧ ∧ ∧
3. Rehearse the target word by saying each syllable out loud.	Say: **"Im / meas / ur / a / ble."**
4. Rehearse the target word as a unit three times or until you can say it automatically without hesitation.	Say immeasurable three times. 1. **"Immeasurable"** 2. **"Immeasurable"** 3. **"Immeasurable"**
5. Rehearse saying the target word aloud in three sentences or until you feel that you will retrieve it consistently.	Rehearse the following three sentences. 1. **"Immeasurable means limitless."** 2. **"The impact of that man's work is immeasurable."** 3. **"The effect of computers is immeasurable."**

Practice Charts for Applying the Syllable-Dividing Strategies

Select a common word that has either caused you or may cause you to have a "Twist of the Tongue" word-finding error. For initial practice only, apply one of the Syllable-Dividing Strategies to this word by completing the following charts.

Visual Syllable-Dividing

Strategy Steps	Fill In the Blanks
1. Identify a target word that is three or more syllables in length.	Target Word = _____
2. Draw a line between each syllable.	_____ / _____ / _____ / _____

Rhythm Syllable-Dividing

Strategy Steps	Fill In the Blanks
1. Identify a target word that is three or more syllables in length.	Target Word = _____
2. As you say each syllable, mark it with a rhythmic tap to emphasize the syllables of the target word	Make rhythmic taps while you say: _____ _____ _____ _____ ^ ^ ^ ^
3. Rehearse the target word by saying each syllable out loud.	Say: _____ _____ _____ _____
4. Rehearse the target word as a unit three times or until you can say it automatically without hesitation.	1. _____ 2. _____ 3. _____
5. Write three sentences with the target word. Rehearse these sentences until you feel that you have overpracticed the target word and will retrieve it consistently.	Rehearse the following three sentences. 1. _____ 2. _____ 3. _____

Same-Sounds Cue Strategy

After you have rehearsed the production of common words, you may also want to use the Same-Sounds Cue to aid your retrieval of these words. The following is an example of how to apply this strategy to words that are three or more syllables in length.

Let's assume you are going to the computer store. You want to explain to the salesman that you want a word-processing software program that will have a good thesaurus. You are worried that you may make a "Twist of the Tongue" word-finding error when you make your request because *thesaurus* is a three-syllable word.

I need software with a good... the...theseres.

Strategy Steps	Example
1. Identify the target word.	Target Word = thesaurus
2. Using the Same-Sounds Cue, link each syllable of the target word with a prompt word that sounds like the syllable.	*Same-Sounds Cue:* Link the syllable / the / to the word *thick* because the word *thick* and the syllable / the / begin with the same sounds (not letters).
	Link the syllable / saur / to the word *sore* because the word *sore* and the syllable / saur / consist of the same sounds.
	Link the syllable / us / to the word *us* because the word *us* and the syllable / us / consist of the same sounds.

Continued on next page

Strategy Steps	Example
3. Review these links between the Same-Sounds Cues and the target word syllables by thinking of the prompt words immediately before saying the target word out loud.	Think of the cues *thick-sore-us* immediately before saying the target word aloud. (…thick-sore-us) **"Thesaurus"**
4. Rehearse application of this strategy in three sentences or until you feel that you have overpracticed the target word and will retrieve it consistently.	Think of the cues immediately before saying the target word aloud in three sentences. 1. **"A** (…thick-sore-us) **thesaurus is available in software."** 2. **"The** (…thick-sore-us) **thesaurus will be helpful."** 3. **"I need to get a** (…thick-sore-us) **thesaurus."**

We visited the …aretum…arber …the place with trees.

Let's assume you were telling your children that you took your class on a field trip. As you related the event, you had difficulty retrieving the noun *arboretum*. To anchor future retrieval of the four-syllable noun *arboretum*, link each syllable with a word that sounds like that syllable. Use the following steps to apply the Same-Sounds Cue Strategy to aid accurate retrieval of the noun *arboretum*.

Strategy Steps	Example
1. Identify the target word.	Target Word = arboretum
2. Using the Same-Sounds Cue, link each syllable of the target word with a prompt word that sounds like the syllable.	*Same-Sounds Cue:* Link the syllables / ar / bor / to the word *harbor* because the word *harbor* and the syllables / ar / bor / consist of some of the same sounds.

Continued on next page

Strategy Steps	Example
	Link the syllable / et / to the word *eat* because the word *eat* and the syllable / et / consist of the same sounds.
	Link the syllable / um / to the cue *um* because the cue *um* and the syllable / um / consist of the same sounds.
3. Review these links between the Same-Sounds Cues and the target word syllables by thinking of the prompt words immediately before saying the target word out loud.	Think of the cues *harbor-eat-um* immediately before saying aloud the target word. (...harbor-eat-um) **"Arboretum"**
4. Rehearse application of this strategy in three sentences or until you feel that you have overpracticed the target word and will retrieve it consistently.	Think of the cues immediately before saying the target word aloud in three sentences. 1. **"The** (...harbor-eat-um) **arboretum is for rare trees."** 2. **"The** (...harbor-eat-um) **arboretum is at the gardens."** 3. **"The** (...harbor-eat-um) **arboretum was interesting."**

Practice Chart for Applying the Same-Sounds Cue Strategy

Select a common noun, verb, adjective, or adverb that has either caused you or may cause you to have a "Twist of the Tongue" word-finding error. For initial practice only, apply the Same-Sounds Cue Strategy to this name by completing the following chart.

Strategy Steps	Fill In the Blanks
1. Identify the target word.	Target Word = _____
2. Using the Same-Sounds Cue, link each syllable of the target word with a prompt word or phrase that sounds like the syllable.	*Same Sounds Cue:* Link _____ (target syllable) to _____ (cue) because the target syllable and the cue word each begin with the same first sounds. Link _____ (target syllable) to _____ (cue) because the target syllable and the cue word each begin with the same first sounds. Link _____ (target syllable) to _____ (cue) because the target syllable and the cue word each begin with the same first sounds. Link _____ (target syllable) to _____ (cue) because the target syllable and the cue word each begin with the same first sounds.
3. Review these links between the Same-Sounds Cues and the target word syllables by thinking of the prompt words immediately before saying the target word out loud.	Think of _____ (cues) immediately before saying _____ (target word) aloud.
4. Write three sentences with the target word. Rehearse applying the Same-Sounds Cue Strategy in these sentences or until you feel that you have overpracticed the target word and will retrieve it consistently.	Think of _____ (cues) immediately before saying _____ (target word) aloud in three sentences. 1. _____ 2. _____ 3. _____

Alternate Word Strategy

In a conversation, if you anticipate you will have difficulty retrieving a multisyllabic word, switch to an alternate word rather than describing the elusive target word.

Let's assume you are telling your partner that you bought yourself a gift. You are having difficulty retrieving all the sounds for the target word *amethyst*.

For example, in this situation rather than describing the color of the stone that you bought, you could switch to a category name. Substitute the word *gemstone* for the target word *amethyst*. Use the following steps to apply the Synonym or Category-Name Substitution Strategy. After the conversation, anchor retrieval of the elusive multisyllabic word with the Same-Sounds Cue Strategy and the Syllable-Dividing Strategies presented previously.

Strategy Steps	Example
1. While you are talking, think ahead to identify a word that you may have trouble retrieving.	Target Word = amethyst
2. Think of a word that is similar in meaning to the elusive word.	gemstone

Continued on next page

Strategy Steps	Example
3. Using the Alternate Word Strategy, substitute a category name for the elusive target word.	Substitute the word *gemstone* for the target word *amethyst*.
4. Complete the sentence inserting the category name in place of the target word while you are talking.	**"I bought myself a beautiful gemstone."**
5. Rehearse application of this strategy prior to an event by thinking of alternate words for target words or names that you think you might have difficulty retrieving.	

Final Guidelines for Applying Strategies to Reduce "Twists of the Tongue"

This chapter presents final guidelines for applying word-finding strategies to reduce "Twists of the Tongue" when you are speaking. Following these guidelines, try the strategies in Chapter 12 to determine which are most appropriate for your word-finding style. Once you determine which strategy helps you say the name or word automatically, use it consistently to aid your retrieval of long names and words.

Final Guidelines

- Identify the specific names and words that you want to retrieve.
- If you have made a "Twist of The Tongue" word-finding error, apply the word-finding strategies to these target names and words as soon as possible after you produced the error.
- If you are preparing for an upcoming event apply the word-finding strategies to those target names and words with which you think you might make a "Twist of the Tongue" word-finding error.
- If you select one of the Syllable-Dividing Strategies, apply the strategy and rehearse the target name or word by saying it several times out loud as a unit and in a sentence.
- If you select the Same-Sounds Cue Strategy, rehearse the target name or word by thinking of the cue (do not say the cue out loud) and saying the target name or word aloud several times alone and in a sentence.

Once you apply these strategies to the target name or word, you will usually have success in saying it automatically in other contexts. However, if you find that you are still having difficulty with that name or word when you are speaking, review and rehearse the chosen strategy.

PART 6

Troubleshooting

Word Finding at Social Functions and Recreational Activities

Participating in conversations at social functions and recreational activities puts a high demand on your word-finding system. Regardless of the event you are attending, you are expected to be a good communicator. Specifically, at social functions you are expected to be fluent, accurate, and clear when

- addressing and referring to family members, colleagues, and friends;
- inquiring about the lives of other guests;
- sharing experiences in your own life; or
- discussing current events.

When attending sporting events you are expected to retrieve the names of the athletes and the vocabulary specific to that activity in your conversations. When visiting museums, galleries, or attending musical events, you are expected to participate in discussions using the names of the artists and the works you have seen. Therefore, prior to a social gathering or recreational activity, use the word-finding strategies in this book and the plans in this chapter to help you prepare for conversations at these social functions.

This chapter presents preparation plans to reduce the potential of having word-finding difficulties at social functions and recreation activities. The plan directs you to think through future conversations, apply word-finding strategies to relevant vocabulary, and rehearse out loud what you hope to discuss at upcoming events. Use the following steps prior to the event.

Preparation Plans to Reduce Potential Word-Finding Difficulties at Upcoming Events

1. For all functions, rehearse **out loud** the names that you will want to retrieve at these events. Include the names of people who will be attending the event, the names of individuals to whom you may want to refer, and the names of individuals who are involved in the activity. For example, if you are going to a movie or a play, rehearse the title and the names of the performers. If you are going to a restaurant, rehearse its name and the name of entrees. If you are meeting someone for coffee, rehearse names of individuals to whom you may

want to refer, individuals in the news, or in your neighborhood, or names of friends or colleagues.

2. For all functions, rehearse **out loud** the vocabulary that is specific to the activity you are attending. For example, if it is a family event, rehearse the key words you think you will be using in your conversations with family members. If it is a sporting event, rehearse the vocabulary that is unique to that sport. If it is a lecture, rehearse the vocabulary relevant to that topic. If it is a movie, rehearse the vocabulary relevant to the story.

3. During this rehearsal process, predict which names and words might be difficult for you to retrieve during conversations at these events. These would be names or words that could potentially cause one or all of the following word-finding errors.

- Predict names which you could interchange producing a "Slip of the Tongue" word-finding error. For proper names, these typically would be names of individuals who have a similar relationship to you and to each other. For example, you may interchange the names of your children or grandchildren, the names of actors or athletes, or the names of political candidates running for office. For common nouns these may be object names (e.g., DVD for CD) or food names (e.g., salmon for swordfish) from the same category, or medicine names that share some of the same sounds or are used for similar aliments (e.g., Advil for aspirin).

- Predict names or words with which you could potentially have a "Tip of the Tongue" experience in your discourse. These could be names of people, places, or things. For example, you may have difficulty retrieving the name of an actor, author, or artist in a conversation about a movie, play, or art exhibit. Or you may have difficulty retrieving the name of a building, city, or country in an upcoming discussion of current events. Or you may have difficulty retrieving the name of a computer or automotive part that you purchased earlier in the day.

- Predict names or words which could potentially cause a "Twist of the Tongue" word-finding error. These would be names or words that are three or more syllables in length. For example, you may have difficulty retrieving long names of actors, authors, or artists in a conversation about a movie, play, or art exhibit. Or you may have difficulty retrieving the names of countries or country leaders in an upcoming discussion of world news or the global economy. Or you may have difficulty retrieving the name of a medicine you are taking or a medical test you are considering because the words are multisyllabic.

4. Accordingly, apply the strategies recommended in this book to each of the words that you predict will be difficult for you to retrieve.

   - As you rehearse your conversations, practice the Pausing Strategy with names or words that potentially may cause a "Slip of the Tongue" word-finding error.

- Link Association Cues to names or words that potentially may cause a "Tip of the Tongue" experience to anchor their retrieval.
- Use Syllable-Dividing Strategies for names or words that potentially may cause a "Twist of the Tongue" word-finding error.

5. While applying strategies to the target names and words, rehearse several times **out loud** the potentially troublesome names and words you plan to use in your conversations. Continue this rehearsal until you feel you will accurately and fluently retrieve the names and words you identified.

Word Finding when Giving Speeches and Presentations and Participating in Meetings

This chapter presents preparation plans for activities that could put a high demand on your word-finding system. Activities discussed include preparing for giving presentations or speeches and participating in meetings.

Preparation Plans to Reduce Word-Finding Errors During Presentations and Speeches

This section presents a preparation plan for using word-finding strategies to reduce potential word-finding errors when giving presentations or speeches. These presentations may be informal or formal and may take place in any one of the following settings.

- business meetings
- school meetings
- political rallies
- religious gatherings
- community hearings
- homeowners association meetings
- neighborhood gatherings

Regardless of the nature of these presentations, the demands on the speaker's word-finding skills are the same. The speaker is expected to be fluent, to be accurate, and to be clear. It is recommend when preparing a presentation or speech, that you use the word-finding strategies in this book and the preparation plans in this chapter to minimize your potential for making word-finding errors during your presentation. Use the following steps prior to your presentation or speech.

1. Write everything you plan to say in your speech or presentation.
2. Rehearse by reading your presentation out loud and circling any words that you might have difficulty retrieving during your presentation. These would be words that could potentially cause one or all of the word-finding errors discussed in this book.

- First, circle words or names that you predict you could interchange producing a "Slip of the Tongue" word-finding error. For proper names, these typically would be names of individuals who have a similar relationship to each other. For example, you may interchange the names of authors, officers, trustees, committee chairs, or staff members. For common nouns, troublesome target words may be names of objects or places that are in the same category. That is, you may interchange the names of computers, locations, or products that you are marketing.

- Predict names or words with which you could potentially have a "Tip of the Tongue" experience in your discourse. Typically, these would be names of people, places, or things. For example, you may have difficulty retrieving the name of a client, an employer, a corporation, or a location that you are discussing. Or you may have difficulty retrieving the name of a form, a product, a document, or an agreement that is under study. Or you may have a "Tip of the Tongue" experience with words describing important people, places, or entities.

- Lastly, predict names or words that could potentially cause a "Twist of the Tongue" word-finding error. These would be names or words that are three or more syllables in length. For example, you may have difficulty retrieving long names of clients, buildings, locations, products, or documents. Or you may have difficulty retrieving multisyllabic descriptive terms like, judicious, conscientious, or capricious.

3. Apply the corresponding strategies recommended in this book to each of the potential word-finding errors that you circled in your presentation.

- As you rehearse your presentation or speech, practice the Pausing Strategy with names or words that potentially may cause a "Slip of the Tongue" word-finding error.

- Link Association Cues to names or words that potentially may cause a "Tip of the Tongue" experience to anchor their retrieval.

- Use Syllable-Dividing Strategies for names or words that potentially may cause a "Twist of the Tongue" word-finding error.

4. While applying these strategies rehearse your presentation or speech **out loud** several times until you are able to recite it or read it without any word finding errors. (Remember to always rehearse **out loud**. Rehearsing silently will not improve your word-finding skills when you are giving your presentation.)

5. Lastly, rehearse your speech or presentation **out loud** just prior to the time when you will be giving your presentation.

Preparation of Visual Aids to Be Used In Your Presentation or Speech.

Create slides or transparencies not only to impart information to the audience, but also to aid your word-finding skills during your presentation.

1. Create transparencies or computer slides that contain the vocabulary, names, and dates that you need to retrieve during the presentation.

2. Create a slide with answers to most frequently asked questions.

3. If using transparencies, put retrieval cues on paper backing of each transparency.

Activities to Reduce Demands on Your Word-Finding System During Presentations or Speeches

Use the following guidelines during your presentation or speech to aid your word-finding skills.

1. Ask members of the audience to wear name tags.

2. Present transparencies or computer slides as you give your presentation using each transparency or slide as a resource to cue your word finding as you speak.

3. Field questions at strategic points in your presentation. You want questions to follow closely after you have presented the content so that your verbalization of key names, dates, and vocabulary has been recent.

4. To cue your retrieval, redisplay transparencies or slides with content corresponding to the questions asked.

5. Ask participants to write questions so that you can read them to the audience before answering them. Reading questions out loud can cue your retrieval of words, names, or facts that you may need to use in your answer.

6. Obtain additional time to respond to unexpected questions when you feel you cannot respond fluently. Indicate to your audience that you will get back to them with your response through voice mail or e-mail.

Follow-Up Activities After the Presentation or Speech

After your presentation use the following recommendations.

1. Apply your retrieval strategies to additional names, dates, or vocabulary that emerged during the presentation.
2. Update your transparencies or computer slides to contain these additional names, dates, and vocabulary.
3. Follow-up through voice mail and e-mail with any answers to questions that you either did not address or did not answer completely during your presentation or speech.

Preparation Plans to Reduce Word-Finding Errors when Talking or Asking Questions at a Meeting

Regardless of the topic or location of a meeting you want to be fluent, accurate, and clear when you voice your opinions or ask questions. However, problems in word finding can interrupt your communication even when your participation is brief. Prior to a meeting, it is important to use the word-finding strategies in this book while you rehearse **out loud** the opinions you are going to share and the questions you are going to ask. Use the following steps prior to the meeting.

1. After reviewing the minutes of the previous meeting and the upcoming agenda, write the questions you plan to ask and the opinions you plan to share at the next meeting.

2. Rehearse the questions you plan to ask and the comments you plan to make, circling any words you predict might be difficult to retrieve during the meeting. These would be words that could cause one or all of word-finding errors highlighted earlier in this chapter.

3. Apply the corresponding strategies recommended in this book to the words you have identified as potentially troublesome.

4. Continue rehearsal of this material until you feel that you will accurately and fluently verbalize the information you want to present.

PART 7

Strategies and Accommodations for Academic- and Work-Related Vocabulary

Word-Finding Strategies for Academic- and Work-Related Vocabulary

"I am 19 years old. My IQ is somewhere around 150 to 160. I have no problems in any class except for English. My understanding of the books we have studied is well above the other students. My thoughts are all there, but I cannot find the words to get them out correctly. All my problems lay within the semantics of the language."

Learners, such as the individual in this example, indicate that they also have difficulty retrieving academic- and work-related vocabulary. Although these individuals report that they learn the meanings of vocabulary quickly, their retrieval of many of these words may never become automatic. Their stories indicate that they experience all three of the word-finding disruptions discussed in this book when they attempt to use academic- and work-related vocabulary. This chapter demonstrates how to apply

175

word-finding strategies to aid retrieval of vocabulary at school or on the job. The following questions are addressed.

- Why do you need to apply word-finding strategies to academic- and work-related vocabulary?
- What are the word-finding strategies that can be used with academic- and work-related vocabulary?

Why Do You Need to Apply Word-Finding Strategies to Academic- and Work-Related Vocabulary?

Word-finding strategies can help to improve an individual's retrieval of academic- and work-related vocabulary. When word-finding skills of this vocabulary are efficient, thinking is not disrupted due to an inability to select or retrieve necessary vocabulary. This enables learners to analyze and interpret content more effectively and to focus on creating new ideas about the content.

Word-Finding Strategies for Academic- and Work-Related Vocabulary

The word-finding strategies presented in this book are appropriate for improving retrieval of academic- and work-related vocabulary. These word-finding strategies include the Association Cue Strategies, the

Syllable-Dividing Strategies, the Rehearsal Strategy, and the Pausing Strategy. Following are examples of how these strategies are applied to improve retrieval of academic- and work-related vocabulary for all learners.

A "Slip of the Tongue"

This section presents examples for applying the Pausing Strategy to reduce "Slips of the Tongue" when retrieving academic- and work-related vocabulary in class or office discussions, in study groups, or in office meetings.

Pausing Strategy

When using the Pausing Strategy, you pause to keep from saying interfering words. These interfering words are usually words that are said in the same context as the target word (e.g., calculator for computer), or in the same category as the target word (e.g., exponent for coefficient), or sound similar to the target word (e.g., impeachable for impeccable). An important aspect of the Pausing Strategy is to apply it strategically. You insert the pause immediately before saying the word you predict you will have difficulty retrieving.

The major religion was Buddhism , ...no, Hinduism.

Let's assume that your World History class is studying the two major religions that helped shape the civilization of India. As you describe these religious influences, you substitute an interfering name, Buddhism, in the same category as the target name, Hinduism.

The following steps utilize the Pausing Strategy to reduce "Slips of the Tongue" when using these terms or other academic vocabulary.

Strategy Steps	Example
1. Identify the target name.	Target Name = Hinduism
2. Rehearse the Pausing Strategy with the target name.	As you prepare to say Hinduism, follow these steps. 1. Pause. 2. Screen out the interfering name, Buddhism. 3. Rehearse the target name, Hinduism, silently. 4. Say Hinduism out loud. (... ~~Buddhism~~, Hinduism) **"Hinduism"**
3. Rehearse the Pausing Strategy in three sentences.	1. (... ~~Buddhism~~, Hinduism) **"Hinduism is a religion in India."** 2. (... ~~Buddhism~~, Hinduism) **"Hinduism is an eastern religion."** 3. (... ~~Buddhism~~, Hinduism) **"Hinduism has millions of followers."**
4. Identify the target name.	Target Name = Buddhism
5. Rehearse the Pausing Strategy with the target name.	As you prepare to say Buddhism, follow these steps. 1. Pause. 2. Screen out the interfering name, Hinduism. 3. Rehearse the target name, Buddhism, silently. 4. Say Buddhism out loud. (... ~~Hinduism~~, Buddhism) **"Buddhism"**
6. Rehearse the Pausing Strategy in three sentences.	1. (... ~~Hinduism~~, Buddhism) **"Buddhism is an eastern religion."** 2. (... ~~Hinduism~~, Buddhism) **"Buddhism is a religion in Asia."** 3. (... ~~Hinduism~~, Buddhism) **"Buddhism emerged in India about 500 B.C."**

Please convert the PC files, no, I mean the Mac files.

Let's assume you are training a new office manager on the computer system. As you explain how to convert files from one platform to the other, you substitute an interfering name in the same category as the target name, PC files for Mac files.

The following steps utilize the Pausing Strategy to reduce "Slips of the Tongue" when retrieving computer-related terms.

Strategy Steps	Example
1. Identify the target name.	Target Name = Mac files
2. Rehearse the Pausing Strategy with the target name.	As you prepare to say Mac files, follow these steps. 1. Pause. 2. Screen out the interfering name, PC files. 3. Rehearse the target name, Mac files, silently. 4. Say Mac files out loud. (...~~PC files~~, Mac files) **"Mac files"**
3. Rehearse the Pausing Strategy in three sentences.	1. (...~~PC files~~, Mac files) **"Mac files are the ones that need to be converted."** 2. (...~~PC files~~, Mac files) **"Mac files are the ones with the graphics."** 3. (...~~PC files~~, Mac files) **"Mac files will require a lot of memory."**

Practice Chart for Applying the Pausing Strategy

Select two words from school- or work-related vocabulary that you may exchange when you are talking causing a "Slip of the Tongue" word-finding error. For initial practice only, apply the Pausing Strategy to these words by completing the following chart.

Strategy Steps	Fill In the Blanks
1. Identify the target name.	Target Name = _____
2. Rehearse the Pausing Strategy with the target name.	As you prepare to say _____ (target name), follow these steps. 1. Pause. 2. Screen out the interfering name, _____ . 3. Rehearse the target name, _____, silently. 4. Say _____ (target name) out loud.
3. Write three sentences with the target name. Rehearse applying the Pausing Strategy in these sentences.	1. _____ 2. _____ 3. _____
4. Identify the target name.	Target Name = _____
5. Rehearse the Pausing Strategy with the target name.	As you prepare to say _____ (target name), follow these steps. 1. Pause. 2. Screen out the interfering name, _____ . 3. Rehearse the target name, _____, silently. 4. Say _____ (target name) out loud.
6. Write three sentences with the target name. Rehearse applying the Pausing Strategy in these sentences.	1. _____ 2. _____ 3. _____

Same-Sounds Cue Strategy

The Same-Sounds Cue can be used to help reduce "Slips of the Tongue" with academic- or work-related vocabulary. To use this strategy, identify word pairs that you think you might incorrectly interchange when talking. Link a Same-Sounds Cue to the target word. Use the following steps to apply this strategy.

Strategy Steps	Example
1. Identify the target names.	Target Names = Hinduism and Buddhism
2. Using the Same-Sounds Cue, link the target name with a prompt word or phrase that sounds like the target name.	*Same-Sounds Cue:* Link Hinduism to the word *hint* because the word *hint* and the name Hinduism each begin with the same sounds. *Same-Sounds Cue:* Link Buddhism to the word *boo* because the word *boo* and the name Buddhism each begin with the same sounds.

3. Review this link between the Same-Sounds Cue and the target name by thinking of the prompt word immediately before saying the target name out loud.	Think of the cue *hint* immediately before saying the target name aloud.
	    (...hint) **"Hinduism"**
	Think of the cue *boo* immediately before saying the target name aloud.
	    (...boo) **"Buddhism"**

4. Rehearse application of this strategy in three sentences or until you feel that you have overpracticed the target name and will retrieve it consistently.	Think of the cue immediately before saying the target word aloud in three sentences. 1. (...hint) **"Hinduism is an Indian religion."** 2. (...hint) **"Hinduism is a religion of India."** 3. (...hint) **"Hinduism has millions of followers."**

Continued on next page

Strategy Steps	Example
	Think of the cue immediately before saying the target name aloud in three sentences. 1. (…boo) **"Buddhism is an Indian religion."** 2. (…boo) **"Buddhism is a religion of India."** 3. (…boo) **"Buddhism emerged in India about 500 B.C."**

A "Tip of the Tongue"

This section presents examples for applying the Association Cue Strategy to prevent a "Tip of the Tongue" experience when retrieving academic- or work-related vocabulary in school or work settings.

Same-Sounds Cue Strategy

A Same-Sounds Cue Strategy is also recommended to improve your retrieval of academic- (e.g., literature, science, history, mathematics, etc.) or work-related vocabulary. When using this strategy to improve your word-finding skills, you link the target word to a cue word that sounds like (shares similar sounds with) the target word.

Examples of particles are …um…electrons and…uh….

Let's assume that you are taking a physics class to fill one of your science requirements. You are studying different kinds of particles. You do not want to have a "Tip of the Tongue" experience in class when you are discussing these concepts.

The following steps utilize the Same-Sounds Cue Strategy to anchor your retrieval of the terms *electrons, protons,* and *neutrons.*

Strategy Steps	Example
1. Identify the target words.	Target Words = electrons, protons, and neutrons
2. Using the Same-Sounds Cue, link the target word with a prompt word or phrase that sounds like the target word.	*Same-Sounds Cue:* Link each target word to a cue word because the cue word and the corresponding target word each begin with the same first sounds. Link the word *electrons* to the cue *elections.* Link the word *protons* to the cue *programs.* Link the word *neutrons* to the cue *news.*
3. Review this link between the Same-Sounds Cue and the target word by thinking of the prompt word immediately before saying the target word out loud.	Think of the cue immediately before saying the target word aloud. (...elections) **"Electrons"** (...programs) **"Protons"** (...news) **"Neutrons"**
4. Rehearse application of this strategy in several sentences or until you feel that you have overpracticed the target word and will retrieve it consistently.	Think of the cue immediately before saying the target word aloud in a sentence. 1. (...elections) **"Electrons are particles."** 2. (...programs) **"Protons are particles."** 3. (...news) **"Neutrons are particles."**

The... the...not the defendant, but the ...um...uh....

Let's assume that you are an attorney preparing for a conference with your colleagues. You do not want to have a "Tip of the Tongue" experience when you are identifying the plaintiff and the defendant in the case.

The following steps utilize the Same-Sounds Cue Strategy to anchor your retrieval of the terms *plaintiff* and *defendant*.

Strategy Steps	Example
1. Identify the target words.	Target Words = plaintiff and defendant
2. Using the Same-Sounds Cue, link the target word with a prompt word or phrase that sounds like the target word.	*Same-Sounds Cue:* Link each target word to a cue word because the cue word and the corresponding target word each begin with the same sounds. Link the word *plain* to the cue *plaintiff*. Link the word *defend* to the cue *defendant*.
3. Review this link between the Same-Sounds Cue and the target word by thinking of the prompt word immediately before saying the target word out loud.	Think of the cue immediately before saying the target word aloud. (…plain) **"Plaintiff"** (…defend) **"Defendant"**
4. Rehearse application of this strategy in several sentences or until you feel that you have overpracticed the target word and will retrieve it consistently.	Think of the cue immediately before saying the target word aloud in a sentence. 1. **"The** (…plain) **plaintiff institutes the suit."** 2. **"The** (…defend) **defendant is the person against whom the suit was brought."** 3. **"The** (…plain) **plaintiff is Mr. Jones."**

Practice Chart for Applying the Same-Sounds Cue Strategy

Select a word from school- or work-related vocabulary that has either caused you or may cause you to have a "Tip of the Tongue" word-finding error. For initial practice only, apply the Same-Sounds Cue Strategy to this word by completing the following chart.

Strategy Steps	Fill In the Blanks
1. Identify the target word.	Target Word = _____
2. Using the Same-Sounds Cue, link the target word with a prompt word or phrase that sounds like the target word.	*Same-Sounds Cue:* Link _____ (target word) to _____ (cue) because the target word and the cue word each begin with the same first sounds.
3. Review this link between the Same-Sounds Cue and the target word by thinking of the prompt word immediately before saying the target word out loud.	Think of _____ (cue) immediately before saying _____ (target word) aloud.
4. Write three sentences with the target word. Rehearse applying the Same-Sounds Cue Strategy in these sentences or until you feel that you have overpracticed the target word and will retrieve it consistently.	Think of _____ (cue) immediately before saying _____ (target word) aloud in the three sentences. 1. _____ 2. _____ 3. _____

Same-Sounds Meaning Cue Strategy

The Same-Sounds Meaning Cue Strategy is also recommended to improve your retrieval of academic- or work-related vocabulary. When using the Same-Sounds Meaning Cue Strategy, you link a cue word(s) with the target word that both sounds like and is linked to the target word in meaning. The following example illustrates how to apply the Same-Sounds Meaning Cue Strategy to improve retrieval of academic- or work-related vocabulary.

The band that connects the hemispheres is the...um....

Let's assume you are taking an Anatomy of the Human Body class and you are studying the central nervous system. Because you are graded on your class participation, you do not want to have a "Tip of the Tongue" experience in class when you are discussing the parts of the brain.

Use the following steps to apply the Same-Sounds Meaning Cue Strategy to anchor your retrieval of anatomy vocabulary and other vocabulary that may be difficult to retrieve.

Strategy Steps	Example
1. Identify the target words.	Target Words = corpus callosum
2. Using the Same-Sounds Meaning Cue, associate the target words with a prompt word or phrase that both sounds like the target words and is linked in meaning to the target words.	*Same-Sounds Cue:* Link corpus with the word *core* because the target word and the cue word consist of the same first sounds. Link callosum with the word *colossal* because the target word and the cue word consist of the same first sounds. *Meaning Cue: Core* is also a meaning cue because core means center or most important and the corpus callosum is the band of fibers central to the connection of the two hemispheres of the brain. *Colossal* is also a meaning cue because colossal means large. The corpus callosum is the large band of fibers that connects the two hemispheres of the brain.

Continued on next page

Strategy Steps	Example
3. Review this link between the Same-Sounds Meaning Cues and the target words by thinking of the prompt words immediately before saying the target words out loud.	Think of the cues *core* and *colossal* before saying corpus callosum aloud. (…core) **"corpus"** (…colossal) **"callosum"**
4. Rehearse application of this strategy in three sentences or until you feel that you have overpracticed the target words and will retrieve them consistently.	Think of the cues immediately before saying the target words aloud in three sentences. 1. **"The** (…core) **corpus** (…colossal) **callosum allows for communication between the hemispheres."** 2. **"Cutting the** (…core) **corpus** (…colossal) **callosum disrupts communication between the hemispheres."** 3. **"The** (…core) **corpus** (…colossal) **callosum is a band of fibers connecting the hemispheres."**

Practice Chart for Applying the Same-Sounds Meaning Cue Strategy

Select a word from school- or work-related vocabulary that has either caused you or may cause you to have a "Tip of the Tongue" word-finding error. For initial practice only, apply the Same-Sounds Meaning Cue Strategy to this word by completing the following chart.

Strategy Steps	Fill In the Blanks
1. Identify the target word.	Target Word = _____
2. Using the Same-Sounds Meaning Cue, associate the target word with a prompt word or phrase that both sounds like the target word and is linked in meaning to the target word.	*Same-Sounds Cue:* Link _____ (target word) to _____ (cue) because the target word and the cue word each begin with the same first sounds.

Continued on next page

Strategy Steps	Fill In the Blanks
	Meaning Cue: _____ is also a meaning cue because _____ .
3. Review this link between the Same-Sounds Meaning Cue and the target word by thinking of the prompt word immediately before saying the target word out loud.	Think of _____ (cue) immediately before saying _____ (target word) aloud.
4. Write three sentences with the target word. Rehearse applying the Same-Sounds Meaning Cue Strategy in these sentences or until you feel that you have overpracticed the target name and will retrieve it consistently.	Think of _____ (cue) immediately before saying _____ (target word) aloud in three sentences. 1. _____ 2. _____ 3. _____

Familiar-Word Cue Strategy

The Familiar-Word Cue can also be used to improve your retrieval of academic- or work-related vocabulary. A Familiar-Word Cue is a cue word(s) that is frequently said (co-occurs) with the target word in other contexts. When using this strategy to improve your word-finding skills, you link this Familiar-Word Cue to the target word.

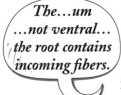

The...um ...not ventral... the root contains incoming fibers.

Let's assume you are teaching an anatomy lesson focused on the spinal cord. You do not want to have a "Tip of the Tongue" experience when you are differentiating the dorsal root from the ventral root for your class.

The following steps utilize the Familiar-Word Cue Strategy to aid your retrieval of the target word *dorsal* as well as other vocabulary.

Strategy Steps	Example
1. Identify the target word.	Target Word = dorsal
2. Using the Familiar-Word Cue, associate the target word with a prompt word that frequently co-occurs with the target word in other contexts.	Link dorsal to the words *dorsal fin* because the word *fin* is often said with the word *dorsal* in a different context.
3. Review this link between the Familiar-Word Cue and the target word by thinking of the prompt word(s) immediately before saying the target word out loud.	Think of the cue *dorsal fin* immediately before saying dorsal root aloud. (…dorsal fin) **"Dorsal root"**
4. Rehearse application of this strategy in three sentences or until you feel that you have overpracticed the target word and will retrieve it consistently.	Think of the cue immediately before saying the target word aloud in three sentences. 1. **"The** (…dorsal fin) **dorsal root contains incoming fibers."** 2. **"The** (…dorsal fin) **dorsal root is different from the ventral root."** 3. **"The** (…dorsal fin) **dorsal root refers to the outer part of the spinal cord."**

A "Twist of the Tongue"

This section presents word-finding strategies to help prevent a "Twist of the Tongue" experience when retrieving academic- or work-related vocabulary. The Visual and Rhythm Syllable-Dividing Strategies and the Same-Sounds Cue Strategy are recommended.

Visual and Rhythm Syllable-Dividing Strategy

To improve retrieval of academic- or work-related vocabulary that is three or more syllables in length, use one of the Syllable-Dividing Strategies. Either draw a line between each syllable (Visual Syllable-Dividing) or mark each syllable with a rhythmic tap (Rhythm Syllable-Dividing) before rehearsing the word. The following example illustrates application of the Syllable-Dividing Strategy to improve retrieval of academic- or work-related vocabulary three or more syllables in length.

Odysseus left the goddess of... Cal...Calso and met...Al....

Let's assume you are taking a literature class to fill one of your English requirements. You are studying epic poetry and have just read *The Odyssey* by Homer. Because class discussion represents a portion of your final grade, you want to be able to explain in class that Odysseus left the goddess Calypso and then met the ruler Alcinous.

Because the names Odysseus, Calypso, and Alcinous are all three- and four-syllable names, you would use the Syllable-Dividing Strategies to ensure correct and automatic retrieval of the names. The following steps utilize the Visual and Rhythm Syllable-Dividing Strategies to aid retrieval of character names in the literature you are reading.

Visual Syllable-Dividing

Strategy Steps	Example
1. Identify the target names.	Target Names = Odysseus, Calypso, and Alcinous
2. Draw a line between the syllables of each name. (Note that some literature texts have already done this for you.)	O / dyss / e / us Ca / lyp / so Al / cin / o / us

Rhythm Syllable-Dividing

Strategy Steps	Example
1. Identify the target names.	Target Names = Odysseus, Calypso, and Alcinous
2. As you say each syllable, mark it with a rhythmic tap to emphasize the syllables of the target word.	Make four rhythmic taps while you say: **"O dyss e us"** ∧ ∧ ∧ ∧ Make three rhythmic taps while you say: **"Ca lyp so"** ∧ ∧ ∧ Make four rhythmic taps while you say: **"Al cin o us"** ∧ ∧ ∧ ∧
3. Rehearse the target names by saying each syllable out loud.	Say: **"O / dyss / e / us"** **"Ca / lyp / so"** **"Al / cin / o / us"**
4. Rehearse the target names as a unit three times or until you can say them automatically without hesitation.	1. **"Odysseus"** 1. **"Calypso"** 1. **"Alcinous"** 2. **"Odysseus"** 2. **"Calypso"** 2. **"Alcinous"** 3. **"Odysseus"** 3. **"Calypso"** 3. **"Alcinous"**
5. Rehearse saying the target names aloud in three sentences or until you feel that you will be able to retrieve them consistently.	1. **"Odysseus, Calypso, and Alcinous are all characters in *The Odyssey*."** 2. **"Odysseus left the goddess Calypso."** 3. **"Alcinous wanted Odysseus to tell of his adventures."**

> *The decision will be made by the...judious...the judiciary.*

Let's assume you are a court reporter and you are explaining to a colleague the make-up of the judiciary. You do not want to have a "Twist of the Tongue" on this multisyllabic word during your conference.

Because the word *judiciary* is a five-syllable word, you would use one of the Syllable-Dividing Strategies to ensure correct and automatic retrieval of this multisyllabic word. The following steps utilize the Visual and Rhythm Syllable-Dividing Strategies to aid retrieval of this legal term.

Visual Syllable-Dividing

Strategy Steps	Example
1. Identify the target word.	Target Word = judiciary
2. Draw a line between each syllable.	Ju / di / ci / ar / y

Rhythm Syllable-Dividing

Strategy Steps	Example
1. Identify the target word.	Target Word = judiciary
2. As you say each syllable, mark it with a rhythmic tap to emphasize the syllables of the target word.	Make five rhythmic taps while you say: **"Ju di ci ar y"** ∧ ∧ ∧ ∧ ∧
3. Rehearse the target word by saying each syllable out loud.	Say: **"Ju / di / ci / ar / y"**
4. Rehearse the target word as a unit three times or until you can say it automatically without hesitation.	1. **"Judiciary"** 2. **"Judiciary"** 3. **"Judiciary"**

Continued on next page

Strategy Steps	Example
5. Rehearse saying the target word aloud in three sentences or until you feel that you will retrieve it consistently.	1. **"The judiciary pertains to the court system."** 2. **"The judiciary is the judicial branch of the government."** 3. **"The judiciary refers collectively to the judges."**

Practice Charts for Applying the Syllable-Dividing Strategies

Select a multisyllabic word from school- or work-related vocabulary that has either caused you or may cause you to have a "Twist of the Tongue" word-finding error. For initial practice only, apply one of the Syllable-Dividing Strategies to this word by completing the following charts.

Visual Syllable-Dividing

Strategy Steps	Fill In the Blanks
1. Identify a target word that is three or more syllables in length.	Target Word = _____
2. Draw a line between each syllable.	____ / ____ / ____ / ____ / ____

Rhythm Syllable-Dividing

Strategy Steps	Fill In the Blanks
1. Identify a target word that is three or more syllables in length.	Target Word = _____
2. As you say each syllable, mark it with a rhythmic tap to emphasize the syllables of the target word	Make rhythmic taps while you say: ____ ____ ____ ____ ∧ ∧ ∧ ∧

Continued on next page

Strategy Steps	Fill In the Blanks
3. Rehearse the target word by saying each syllable out loud.	Say: _____ _____ _____ _____
4. Rehearse the target word as a unit three times or until you can say it automatically without hesitation.	1. _____ 2. _____ 3. _____
5. Write three sentences with the target word. Rehearse these sentences until you feel that you have overpracticed the target word and will retrieve it consistently.	Rehearse the following three sentences. 1. _____ 2. _____ 3. _____

Same-Sounds Cue Strategy

The Same-Sounds Cue Strategy can be used to reduce "Twists of the Tongue" with academic- or work-related vocabulary that is three or more syllables in length. When using this strategy to improve your word-finding skills of long words or names, link each syllable to a word that sounds like that syllable. The following examples illustrate application of the Same-Sounds Cue Strategy to improve retrieval of academic- and work-related vocabulary words that are three or more syllables in length.

One of the words I selected was… in…adve…uh.

Let's assume you are taking a speech class. Professor Roberts expects you to include two or more abstract words in your presentation. *Inadvertently* is one of the words you selected.

To avoid having a "Twist of the Tongue" experience with this target word, use the Same-Sounds Cue Strategy to ensure that your retrieval will be automatic. Use the following steps to ensure fluent retrieval of this target word.

Strategy Steps	Example
1. Identify the target word.	Target Word = inadvertently
2. Using the Same-Sounds Cue, link the syllables of the target word with prompt words that sound like the syllables.	*Same-Sounds Cue:* Link the syllable / in / to the word *in* because the word *in* and the syllable / in / consist of the same sounds. Link the syllables / ad / ver / to the word *adverb* because the word *adverb* and the syllables / ad / ver / consist of the same sounds. Link the syllable / tent / to the word *tent* because the word *tent* and the syllable / tent / consist of the same sounds. Link the syllable / ly / to the name Lee because the name Lee and the syllable / ly / consist of the same sounds.
3. Review these links between the Same-Sounds Cue and the target word syllables by thinking of the prompt words immediately before saying the target word out loud.	Think of the cues *in-adverb-tent-lee* immediately before saying the target word aloud. (…in-adverb-tent-lee) **"Inadvertently"**
4. Rehearse application of this strategy in three sentences or until you feel that you have overpracticed the target word and will retrieve it consistently.	Think of the cues immediately before saying the target word aloud in three sentences. 1. **"She** (…in-adverb-tent-lee) **inadvertently left a voice message."** 2. **"She** (…in-adverb-tent-lee) **inadvertently skipped a question."** 3. **"She** (…in-adverb-tent-lee) **inadvertently forgot to sign in."**

Rehearsal Strategy

The Rehearsal Strategy involves rehearsing the academic- or work-related vocabulary by saying them aloud in isolation and in three sentences. *Do not say* the chosen cue out loud. Think of the cue and then say the target name or word aloud. Remember to always rehearse **out loud**. Rehearsing silently will not improve your word-finding skills when you are talking. Because the Rehearsal Strategy is used with all the word-finding strategies presented, application of this strategy is indicated with each of the word-finding strategies.

Word-Finding Accommodations in Academic and Work Settings

" I'm almost always searching for words even the most simple words like *door* or *chair*. It is not like I don't know these words. They are just always at the edge of my mind and I can't reach them. It does affect my work and people sometimes think I have no idea what I'm talking about even though I do. "

This individual is concerned about her word-finding difficulties. She could benefit from using the following accommodations at work.

This chapter presents accommodations to aid individuals with word-finding difficulties in academic and work settings. These accommodations are used with the retrieval strategies presented earlier in this book to reduce word-finding errors when engaged in academic- or work-related activities. The following questions are addressed.

- What are accommodations for word finding?
- What are helpful word-finding accommodations for academic settings?
- What are helpful word-finding accommodations for work settings?

What Are Accommodations for Word Finding?

Accommodations for word finding are changes or modifications that you make in your communication environment to reduce stress on your word-finding system. These accommodations aid you when you are talking. If you are an individual who frequently has difficulties with word finding, empower yourself to create and use these word-finding accommodations to facilitate your communication at school or work.

What Are Helpful Word-Finding Accommodations for Academic Settings?

In academic settings, accommodations are "best practice" for learners who frequently have difficulties with word finding. The purpose of these accommodations is to provide students with support in the classroom when they are expressing their ideas, doing assignments, and taking exams. All of the accommodations listed are directed toward relieving the word-finding demands inherent in the academic setting. These academic-related accommodations are focused on three areas: school vocabulary, classroom participation, and assignments and exams.

School Vocabulary

Retrieving school vocabulary can be challenging for students who have difficulties with word finding. If you are such a learner, apply the strategies presented in Chapter 16 to the vocabulary under study. To accomplish this in a timely manner, request vocabulary lists that will be important in upcoming class discussions or will be on exams at the beginning of each content unit. This will allow you to apply word-finding strategies to content vocabulary early in your study.

Classroom Participation

"I hope, he doesn't call on me. **"**

This learner is concerned about her ability to retrieve known answers when called on in class.

If you are taking a course that involves class participation, you may need accommodations to reduce the retrieval demands on your oral language and enable you to share your knowledge of the topic under study. If so, take time to explain to the instructor that you would like to create accommodations to facilitate your participation in class discussions. Following are some accommodations you may want to consider.

- Create alternatives to oral participation in class. For example, prepare an outline or other documentation of content discussed in class. Turn in this unsolicited material to the professor to indicate your understanding of the content discussed.

- Make arrangements with your professor to be called on when you volunteer. This ensures that you have had an opportunity to rehearse the content and are thus, ready to participate.

- When called on in class, ask the professor for choices of answers (multiple choice) if you feel you may have a word-finding disruption.

- During the class discussions, refer to prepared notes (hard copy or electronic) of the important facts and key vocabulary that you may need to retrieve.

- Rather than saying, "I don't know" or, "I pass" when experiencing word-finding blocks, request extended time to answer questions by saying, "Let me reflect or think for a moment before I answer."

Exams and Assignments

"In this class, I need multiple choice, big time!"

This learner is concerned about his ability to retrieve known answers to exam questions in this class.

Certain types of assignments or exams put a significant demand on retrieval skills. For example, test questions requiring retrieval of specific vocabulary, dates, names, and facts can be problematic to individuals with word-finding difficulties. In the testing situation, a problem remembering answers to questions may occur even though you studied the information and know the material being tested. To ensure that an assignment or test is focused on assessing your knowledge of the material rather than your ability to retrieve the content, ask your professor to join with you to create the following exam accommodations.

- Along with your instructor, create an out of class "open book exam." This allows you to refer to text or reference books when answering test questions.
- Ask permission to create a portfolio containing different types of assessments to serve as class evaluations.
- Ask permission to create resource material (hard copy or electronic file) to support your word retrieval on tests or assignments in class.
- Discuss with your professor the feasibility of extending time to complete tests assignments.
- Discuss with your professor the feasibility of modifying test questions to use multiple choice, true and false, or select the answer formats.

What Are Helpful Word-Finding Accommodations for Work Settings?

Typically, individuals who have difficulties with word finding have problems retrieving information on demand, sharing ideas, or responding to questions at work. Therefore, it is important to create accommodations in the work setting to foster successful expression of your ideas. Although the nature of the word-finding accommodations will vary depending on your role at work, all accommodations should focus on relieving the demands on your word-finding system inherent in your work environment. The following accommodations are focused on reducing the word-finding demands inherent in two work contexts: phone conferencing and participating in meetings. These accommodations are also applicable in other work settings. See Chapter 15 for accommodations to reduce demands on your word-finding system when giving presentations and speeches.

Telephone Conferencing

The following accommodations will aid your word-finding skills while on the telephone. They are organized according to how and when you create and use them.

Before the telephone conference, create a cue card or electronic file containing the following information for each telephone conference:

- names of any individuals, places, and dates that you may refer to during the phone conference;
- business topics you plan to discuss along with the key vocabulary you plan to use for each topic; and
- a preselected informal topic you plan to initiate and the vocabulary you plan to use.

During the telephone conference, use the following the guidelines.

- Place the cue card or computer file that you have developed before you. Refer to it to cue your retrieval as needed.
- Write any new information shared, circling names, vocabulary, and dates that you will need for questions or for your summary.
- Take the lead to initiate any non-business conversation on a topic you have already documented on your cueing material and that you have rehearsed.
- Obtain additional time to respond to unexpected questions when you feel you cannot respond fluently. Indicate to your listener or colleague that you will get back to them with your response through voice mail or e-mail.

After the telephone conference, use the following recommendations.

- As needed, apply your retrieval strategies to any additional names or vocabulary that emerged during the telephone conference.

- Update your cueing material to include these additional names, vocabulary, or dates for the next telephone conference.
- Follow-up through voice mail or e-mail with answers to questions that either you did not address or did not answer completely during the phone conference. Use transition phrases such as, "I wanted to follow-up on our conversation..." or "I was rethinking what I said and...."

Participating in Meetings

Regardless of what work you do, you most likely participate in meetings. Whether these are staff meetings, faculty meetings, sales meetings, union meetings, or board meetings, you are expected to ask questions, share ideas, and provide answers. Indicated in this section are accommodations to aid your word-finding skills during these meetings. The accommodations are organized according to those created prior to the meeting, those used during the meeting, and those used after the meeting.

Before the meeting, create a cue card or computer file containing the following information:

- names of all individuals who will be attending the meeting;
- topics that are on the agenda including the names, vocabulary, and dates important to each topic; and
- a list of points you plan to make or a list of questions you plan to ask including any names, key vocabulary, and important dates you plan to use.

During the meeting, use the following guidelines to reduce word-finding difficulties.

- Ask participants to wear nametags or create name charts of individuals attending meetings.
- Place the cue card or computer file that you have developed before you. Refer to your word-finding resource to cue your retrieval when answering or asking questions and when bringing up new topics or ideas.
- Write any new information shared, circling names, vocabulary, and dates that you will want to use in your discussion or in questions.
- Obtain additional time to respond to unexpected questions at the meeting when you feel you cannot respond fluently. Indicate to your audience that you will get back to them with your response through voice mail or e-mail.

After the meeting, use the following guidelines to update your accommodations for future meetings.

- Apply your retrieval strategies to any additional or new names or vocabulary that emerged during the meeting.
- Update your cueing material to include these additional names, vocabulary, or dates for the next meeting.
- Follow-up through voice mail and e-mail with answers to questions that you either did not address or did not answer completely during the meeting.

Use transition phrases such as, "I wanted to follow up on our conversation…" or, "I was rethinking what I said and…."

References

Bloom, P. (Ed.). (1994). *Language Acquisition.* Cambridge, MA: MIT Press.

Bock, K., & Levelt, W. (1994). Language production: Grammatical endocing. In M. A. Gernsbacher (Ed.), *Handbook of psycholinguistics* (pp. 945–983). San Diego: Academic Press.

Brown, R., & McNeill, D. (1966). The "tip of the tongue" phenomenon. *Journal of Verbal Learning and Verbal Behavior, 5,* 325–337.

Burke, D. M., MacKay, D. G., Worthley, J. S., & Wade, E. (1991). On the tip of the tongue: What causes word-finding failures in young and older adults? *Journal of Memory and Language, 30,* 542–579.

Butterworth, B. (1980). Some constraints on models of language production. In B. Butterworth (Ed.), *Language production: Vol. 1. Speech and talk* (pp. 423–459). London: Academic Press.

Butterworth, B. (1981). Speech errors: Old data in search of new theories. *Linguisitcs, 19,* 627–662.

Butterworth, B. (1989). Lexical access in speech production. In W. Marslen-Wilson (Ed.), *Lexical representation and process* (pp. 108–135). Cambridge: Blackwell.

Butterworth, B. (1993). Disorders of phonological encoding. In W. J. M. Levelt (Ed.), *Lexical access in speech production* (pp. 261–286). Cambridge, MA: MIT Press.

Caramazza, A., & Hillis, A. E. (1991). Lexical organization of nouns and verbs in the brain. *Nature, 349,* 788–790.

Coady, J., & Huckin, T. (Eds.). (1997). *Second language vocabulary acquisition.* The Cambridge Applied Linguistics Series. New York: Cambridge University Press.

Conca, L. (1989). Strategy choice by LD children with good and poor naming ability in a naturalistic memory situation. *Learning Disabilities Quarterly, 12,* 92–106.

Dell, G. (1986). A spreading activation theory of retrieval in sentence production. *Psychological Review, 93,* 283–321.

Deshler, D. D., Ellis, E. S., & Lenz, K. B. (1996). *Teaching adolescents with learning disabilities: Strategies and methods.* Denver, CO: Love Publishing.

Fay, D., & Cutler, A. (1977). Malapropisms and the structure of the mental lexicon. *Linguistic Inquiry, 8,* 505–520.

Fromkin, V. A. (Ed.). (1973). *Speech errors as linguistic evidence.* The Hague: Mouton.

Fromkin, V. A. (Ed.). (1980). *Errors in linguistic performance: Slips of the tongue, ear, pen, and hand.* San Diego: Academic Press.

Garrett, M., (1993). Disorders of lexical selection. In W. J. M. Levelt (Ed.), *Lexical access in speech production* (pp. 143–180). Cambridge, MA: Blackwell.

German, D. J. (1990). *Test of Adolescent/Adult Word Finding.* Austin, TX: Pro-Ed.

German, D. J. (1993). *Word-finding intervention program.* Austin, TX: Pro-Ed.

Goodglass, H., & Wingfield, A. (1997). Word-finding deficits in aphasia: Brain-behavior relations and clinical symptomatology. In H. Goodglass & A. Wingfield (Eds.), *Anomia, neuroanatomical, and cognitive correlates* (pp. 3–27). San Diego: Academic Press.

Harrell, M., Parenté, F., Bellingrath, E., & Lisicia, R. (1992). *Cognitive rehabilitation of memory: A practical guide.* Gaithersburg, MD: Aspen Publishers.

Higbee, K. L. (1993). *Your memory, how it works and how you improve it.* New York: Paragon House.

Jones, H. G. V. (1989). Back to Woodworth: Role of interlopers in the tip-of-the-tongue phenomenon. *Memory and Cognition, 17,* 69–76.

Jones, H. G. V., & Langford, S. (1987). Phonological blocking in the tip of the tongue state. *Cognition, 26,* 115–122.

Koriat, A., & Lieblich, I. (1974). What does a person in a "TOT" state know that a person in a "don't know" state doesn't know? *Memory and Cognition, 2*(4), 647–655.

Lerner, J. W. (2000). *Learning disabilities, theories, diagnosis, and teaching strategies* (8th ed.). Boston: Houghton Mifflin.

Lesser, R. (1989). Some issues in the neuropsychological rehabilitation of anomia. In X. Seron & G. Deloche (Eds.), *Cognitive approahes in neuropsychological rehabilitation* (pp. 65–104). Mahwah, NJ: Lawrence Erlbaum Associates.

Levelt, W. J. M. (1989). *Speaking, from intention to articulation.* Cambridge, MA: MIT Press.

Levelt, W. J. M. (1993). Lexical access in speech. In W. J. M. Levelt (Ed.), *Lexical access in speech production* (pp. 1–22). Cambridge, MA: Blackwell.

Lorayne, H., & Lucas, J. (1974). *The memory book.* New York: Ballantine Books.

Mastropieri, M. A., & Scruggs, T. E. (1991). *Teaching students ways to remember: Strategies for learning mnemonically.* Cambridge, MA: Brookline.

McKeown, M. G., & Curtis, M. E. (Eds.). (1987). *The nature of vocabulary acquisition.* Mahwah, NJ: Lawrence Erlbaum Associates.

Meyer, A. S. (1993). Investigations of phonological encoding through speech error analyses: Achievements, limitations, and alternatives. In W. J. M. Levelt (Ed.), *Lexical access in speech production* (pp. 1–22). Cambridge, MA: Blackwell.

Meyer, A. S., & Bock, K. (1992). The tip-of-the-tongue pheonmenon: Blocking or partial activation. *Memory and Cognition, 20,* 715–726.

Nicholas, M., Barth, L. K., Obler, L. K., Au, R., & Albert, M. L. (1997). Naming in normal aging and dementia of the alzheimer's type. In H. Goodglass & A. Wingfield (Eds.), *Anomia, neuroanatomical, and cognitive correlates* (pp. 166–188). San Diego: Academic Press.

Parenté, R., & Herrmann, D. (1996). *Retraining cognition, techniques and applications.* Gaithersburg, MD: Aspen Publishers.

Pinker, S. (1995). *The language instinct: How the mind creates language.* New York: Harper Collins.

Pressley, M., & Woloshyn, V. (Eds.). (1995) *Cognitive strategy instruction that really improves children's academic performance.* Cambridge, MA: Brookline.

Roelofs, A. (1993). A spreading-activation theory of lemma retrieval in speaking. In W. J. M. Levelt (Ed.), *Lexical access in speech production,* (pp. 107–142). Cambridge, MA: Blackwell.

Semenza, C. (1997). Proper-name-specific aphasias. In H. Goodglass & A. Wingfield (Eds.), *Anomia, neuroanatomical, and cognitive correlates* (pp. 115–134). San Diego: Academic Press.

Shallice, T., & Butterworth, B. (1977). Short-term memory impairment and spontaneous speech. *Neuropychologia, 15,* 729–735.

Shattuck-Hufnagel, S. (1993). The role of word structure in segmental serial ordering. In W. J. M. Levelt (Ed.), *Lexical access in speech production* (pp. 213–259). Cambridge, MA: Blackwell.

Trudeau, K. (1995). *Kevin Trudeau's mega memory.* New York: Quill William Morrow.

Index

academic settings (*see* academic
    vocabulary;
    accommodations)

academic vocabulary
  academic settings
    accommodations
      classroom participation,
        199–200
      exams and assignments,
        200–201
      school vocabulary, 199
  Slip of the Tongue
    Pausing Strategy, 177–180
    Same-Sounds Cue Strategy,
      181–182
  Tip of the Tongue
    Familiar-Word Cue Strategy,
      188–189
    Same-Sounds Cue Strategy,
      182–185
    Same-Sounds Meaning Cue
      Strategy, 185–188
  Twist of the Tongue
    Rehearsal Strategy, 196
    Rhythm Syllable-Dividing
      Strategy, 190–194
    Same-Sounds Cue Strategy,
      194–195
    Visual Syllable-Dividing
      Strategy, 190–194

accommodations
  academic settings
    classroom participation,
      199–200
    exams and assignments,
      200–201

    school vocabulary, 199
  word finding, 198
  work settings
    participating in meetings,
      204–206
    telephone conferencing,
      202–204

additional reading
  Slip of the Tongue, 15
  Tip of the Tongue, 19
  Twist of the Tongue, 24
  vocabulary acquisition and
    usage, 55

Alternate Word. *See* Synonym or
    Category-Name Substituting
    Strategy

Association Cueing
  definition, 40–41
  Familiar-Word Cue Strategy
    definition, 45
    steps to use, 45–46
    when to use, 46
  Same-Sounds Cue Strategy
    definition, 41
    steps to use, 41–42
    when to use, 42
  Same-Sounds Meaning Cue
    Strategy
    definition, 42–44
    steps to use, 44
    when to use, 45

characteristics
  Slip of the Tongue, 6, 14–15,
    32–33
  Tip of the Tongue, 7, 18–19,
    33–34
  Twist of the Tongue, 7–8, 23–24,
    35

proper names (*continued*)
    Same-Sounds Meaning Cue
        Strategy, 92–96
    Twist of the Tongue
        Same-Sounds Cue Strategy,
            133–137
        Syllable-Dividing Strategies,
            130–133

recreational activities
    participating in conversations,
        159–163
    preparing for, 160–163
        Slip of the Tongue, 161
        Tip of the Tongue, 162
        Twist of the Tongue, 162
    Rehearsal Strategy, 160–163

Rehearsal Strategy
    academic vocabulary, 196
    definition, 53–54
    participating in meetings, 171
    presentations, 166–168
    recreational activities, 160–163
    Slip of the Tongue, 64
    social functions, 160–163
    speeches, 166–168
    steps to use, 54
    Tip of the Tongue, 92
    Twist of the Tongue, 128–130,
        196
    when to use, 54
    work-related vocabulary, 196

Rhythm Syllable-Dividing Strategy
    academic vocabulary, 190–194
    definition, 48
    steps to use, 48–49
    Twist of the Tongue, 128,
        190–194
    work-related vocabulary,
        190–194

Same-Sounds Cue Strategy
    academic vocabulary, 181–185,
        194–195
    common words, 111–112,
        149–152

definition, 41
names of places, events, and
    entities, 101–103, 107–108,
    142–144
proper names, 133–137
steps to use, 41–42
Slip of the Tongue, 181–182
Tip of the Tongue, 90, 101–103,
    107–108, 111–112, 182–185
Twist of the Tongue, 128,
    133–137, 142–144, 149–152,
    194–195
when to use, 42
work-related vocabulary,
    181–185, 194–195

Same-Sounds Meaning Cue Strategy
    academic vocabulary, 185–188
    common words, 113–114
    definition, 42–44
    names of places, events, and
        entites, 103–105
    proper names, 69–72, 92–96
    Slip of the Tongue, 62–63, 69–72
    steps to use, 44
    Tip of the Tongue, 90, 92–96,
        103–105, 113–114, 185–188
    when to use, 45
    work-related vocabulary,
        185–188

school vocabulary (*See*
    accommodations)

Self-Correction Strategy
    common words, 81
    definition, 52
    Slip of the Tongue, 64, 81
    steps to use, 53
    when to use, 53

Self-Evaluation, 29–35

Slip of the Tongue
    academic vocabulary
        Pausing Strategy, 177–180
        Same-Sounds Cue Strategy,
            181–182

It's on the Tip of My Tongue

Word-Finding Strategies to Remember Names and Words You Often Forget

TOLL FREE FAX TO: 1-866-808-5290 (credit card orders only)

MAIL TO: Word Finding Materials, P.O. Box 64456,
Chicago, IL 60664-0456

Quantity	Price Per Unit	Total
_____ X	$24.95	_____
	TAX (IL res. only) 6.5 %	+ _____
	Sub Total	_____
S&H 10% of Book Price ($5.00 min.)*		+ _____
	Total Included	_____

*Shipping & Handling

If Book Total Is	$24.95	$49.90	$74.85	$99.80	$124.75
Please Add	$5.00	$5.00	$7.48	$9.98	$12.48
If Book Total Is	$149.70	$174.65	$199.60	$224.55	$249.50
Please Add	$14.97	$17.47	$19.96	$22.46	$24.95

Payment

○ VISA # _____ Expires _____

○ MC # _____ Expires _____

○ Check Enclosed / Amount of $ _____

Signature _____

Ship To: (Please Print)

Name _____

Address _____ Apt.# _____

City _____ State _____ Zip _____